Creative
Embellishments
for Gourd Art

Schiffer Publishing Ltd
4880 Lower Valley Road • Atglen, PA 19310

Marianne Barnes

Dedication

This book is dedicated to my son, Mike, and his family. Mike has Multiple Sclerosis (MS) and is in a wheelchair, but his spirit and attitude are incredible. He not only works a full-time job, but he is also a part-time pastor. He loves the Lord with all his heart and that love is reflected throughout his life in many ways. His book, *Dealing with the Diagnosis*, details living and coping with his condition. He offers inspiration to other individuals dealing with MS and helps them to accomplish their goals. When I am discouraged, I just remember what he goes through each day and that he never gives up. With the Lord's help, I can keep going each day too. He also gave me the most wonderful and humble daughter-in-law, Karen, and two incredible grandchildren, Michaela and Marissa. Thanks, son.

Copyright © 2013 by Marianne Barnes

Library of Congress Control Number: 2013956177

All rights reserved. No part of this work may be reproduced or used in any form or by any means—graphic, electronic, or mechanical, including photocopying or information storage and retrieval systems—without written permission from the publisher.

The scanning, uploading, and distribution of this book or any part thereof via the Internet or via any other means without the permission of the publisher is illegal and punishable by law. Please purchase only authorized editions and do not participate in or encourage the electronic piracy of copyrighted materials. "Schiffer," "Schiffer Publishing, Ltd. & Design," and the "Design of pen and inkwell" are registered trademarks of Schiffer Publishing, Ltd.

Designed by Danielle D. Farmer
Type set in Constantia/MrBlaketon

ISBN: 978-0-7643-4492-3
Printed in China

Published by Schiffer Publishing, Ltd.
4880 Lower Valley Road
Atglen, PA 19310
Phone: (610) 593-1777; Fax: (610) 593-2002
E-mail: Info@schifferbooks.com

For our complete selection of fine books on this and related subjects, please visit our website at www.schifferbooks.com.
You may also write for a free catalog.

This book may be purchased from the publisher. Please try your bookstore first.

We are always looking for people to write books on new and related subjects. If you have an idea for a book, please contact us at proposals@schifferbooks.com.

Schiffer Publishing's titles are available at special discounts for bulk purchases for sales promotions or premiums. Special editions, including personalized covers, corporate imprints, and excerpts can be created in large quantities for special needs.
For more information, contact the publisher.

Other Schiffer Books by the Author:
Weaving on Gourds, 978-0-7643-3565-5, $19.99
New and Different Materials for Weaving & Coiling, 978-0-7643-3992-9, $29.99

Other Schiffer Books on Related Subjects:
Antler Art for Baskets and Gourds, 978-0-7643-3615-7, $19.99
Coiled Designs for Gourd Art, 978-0-7643-3011-7, $14.99

Contents

Acknowledgments	4
Introduction	5
Embellishing Your Gourd	**6**
Beads	7
Cabochons and Glass	9
Stone	10
Philodendron Sheath, Pods, and	
Other Natural Materials	11
Antlers	14
Recycled Gourds	15
TUTORIALS & PATTERNS	16
Gourd Vase with Inset Pebbles	16
Tipi	17
Antler Bowl with Horse Hair	19
Ammonite Gourd	20
Gourds with Wire Shapes	21
GALLERY	28
Masks	**40**
Making a Mask	41
GALLERY OF MASKS	44
GALLERY	48
Dolls and Whimsical Gourds	**55**
Wild Women of Gourdonia	56
TUTORIALS & PATTERNS	58
Wild Woman Pin	58
GALLERY	60

Gourd Jewelry	**65**
TUTORIALS & PATTERNS	66
Scrap Gourd Lady Pins	66
Gourd Shard Pins	70
Holiday Gourds	**73**
TUTORIALS & PATTERNS	74
Mouse Christmas Ornament	74
Giraffe and Zebra Ornaments	78
Reindeer	83
Christmas Pickle Ornament	86
GALLERY	88
Folk Art, Recycled, & Old World Angels	**96**
TUTORIALS & PATTERNS	97
Folk Art Angel	97
Recycled Angels	102
Old World Angels	105
Knots	**106**
TUTORIALS & PATTERNS	107
Cross Knot and Turtle Shell Knot	107
Gallery of Completed Projects	110
Biographies of Contributing Artists	112
Suppliers	127
Resources	128

Acknowledgments

I would like to acknowledge my husband, my best cheerleader and helper. My travelin' Gourdettes have encouraged me and given me a party after every book published. My gourd patch has also been great, providing me with information and pictures for this new book, and I would like to acknowledge my online gourd friends who have shared information and photographs for all the books I have written. Thank you to Schiffer Publishing, Ltd., who has made writing my books a wonderful experience. I appreciate their attention to detail and the magnificent way they design their books. Becky Folsom and Charlotte Durrence were so wonderful to read and proof my book. Thank you so much! And last of all, I must mention the best photographer ever, Kelly Hazel!

TOP LEFT AND RIGHT:

Ghost Creek Gourds brought lots of gourd varieties to the Mountain Gourd Gathering in Cedar Mountain, North Carolina. This is an annual August event. *Photography by Kelly Hazel.*

Gail Bishop used a pine needle rim for her carved gourd and beads for embellishment. *Courtesy of Gail Bishop.*

BOTTOM RIGHT:

The author used beads and a wooden fish to embellish her dream catcher on a whole gourd. *Photography by Kelly Hazel.*

Introduction

The gourd is a wonderful pallet for all types of arts and crafts. There are so many shapes, kinds, and color patterns created by the mold that forms on the skin of the hard-shell gourd. The techniques you can use are endless and there is a vast array of materials available for decorating crafty, cute gourds or making serious gourd art. My first book was for those who like to weave on gourds. The second book covered all types of materials that can be used for weaving and coiling — natural and man-made. This book is about embellishments.

Embellishments add fun to the gourd. They bring the gourd to "life." There are chapters on masks, fun and whimsical gourds, jewelry, holiday, and cut and whole gourds in which a variety of embellishments were added.

If you have just started working with gourds, then this is a great book for you. It has so many patterns and tutorials with diagrams and photographs that it will provide plenty of options. All I ask is that you do not copy the patterns and use them for classes or sell them. Make the gourd projects for yourself and use the patterns and tutorials to learn. The artists who submitted the patterns are very generous, but many of them make a living selling their creations at stores and craft shows. They also teach at many gourd events. Always give the artist the credit for their original ideas.

For the experienced gourd artist, you will find some more advanced patterns and ideas to keep you busy. The gallery of completed projects will give you endless ideas and spark your creativity. There is also an extensive list of suppliers to find exactly what you need for decorating and embellishing your gourds.

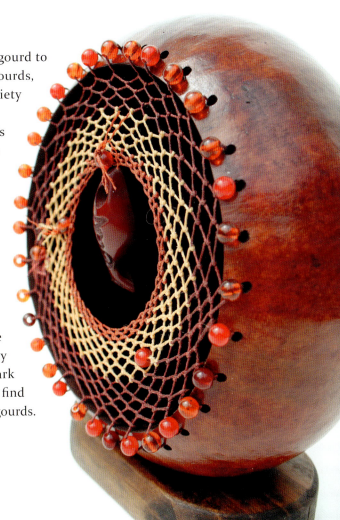

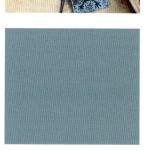

Embellishing Your Gourd

Embellishments put the "wow" in gourd design. There are endless numbers of items that can be used to embellish gourds. A trip outdoors leads to sticks, cactus pad skeletons, vines, roots, feathers, horsehair, antlers, pods, pine cones, seeds, and many more. There are many suppliers who carry all types of embellishments. Here is a list of some embellishments that can be used on gourds: metal feathers, metal cones, beads, conchos, Chinese coins, upholstery tacks, chop sticks, porcupine quills, arrowheads, bones, buffalo teeth, bone washers, dichroic glass cabochons, heishi beads, ammonite fossils, stone cabochons, wire, wire mesh, shells, starfish, clays, Apoxie sculpt, nails, copper, lids, charms, silk flowers, jewelry, buttons, recyclables, cording, rope, glass, and anything you might happen upon.

LEFT:

Bonnie Gibson's cannonball gourd with bone and hematite beads. *Courtesy of Bonnie Gibson.*

Beads

Beads are common embellishments that are used with great success. Since there are various kinds of beads, the colors, textures, sizes, and composition often enhance the gourd design.

TOP AND BOTTOM:

Cookie Hanson's woven rim with bead embellishment. *Courtesy of Cookie Hanson.*

Pine needle rim by Gail Bishop. *Courtesy of Gail Bishop.*

Fish Dream by Marianne Barnes. I love to make dreamcatchers on my gourds. In my first book, *Weaving on Gourds*, there is a pattern for making dreamcatchers. I often add them to a bowl gourd on which I weave a rim. Here I took a different approach with a whole gourd. A hole for the dreamcatcher was cut in the gourd and a bead was stitched in each hole before beginning the dreamcatcher. *Photography by Kelly Hazel.*

Cabochons and Glass

Dichroic glass and stone cabochons can be attached to a gourd or inlaid in a gourd. The flat bottom-round top floral glass beads are easily inlaid. You can find these at a florist or the floral section of a craft store.

TOP:

Inlaid dichroic glass cabochons in the gourd art, titled *Siren*, by Marianne Barnes. *Photography by Kelly Hazel.*

BOTTOM LEFT AND RIGHT:

Cookie Hanson's woven rim with bead embellishment. *Courtesy of Cookie Hanson.*

Gail Bishop inlaid glass cabochons in her faux-leather tooling-gourd. *Courtesy of Gail Bishop.*

Stone

Stone charms, stone chips, and stone donuts are interesting embellishments that can be found online or in most craft stores.

TOP LEFT AND RIGHT:

Iris Durand hanging stone from knotless netting rim. *Photography by Kelly Hazel.*

Kristy Dial used a stone donut embellishment. *Courtesy of Kristy Dial.*

BOTTOM:

Kristy Dial's horsehair rim with emobssed embellishment. *Courtesy of Kristy Dial.*

Philodendron Sheath, Pods, and Other Natural Materials

I love to add natural embellishments to my gourd art. I think the colors and textures create a special look. Betsey Sloan is "The Pod Lady." Her website, www.thepodlady.com, has many unusual pods and botanicals. I see her at festivals in The South and take advantage of shopping for pods that are not native to South Carolina. My personal favorites are Arti Pods and Elephant Ear pods from Brazil, Flower Mushrooms from Australia, and Frog Mouth pods from South America. Betsey also carries some interesting botanicals, such as Ata Fruit Slice from India, Cholla (Dried Cactus) from the USA, and Tall Horn and Bark Butterfly Slices from India. My favorite pod is the jacaranda pod, which is very effective atop a philodendron sheath. Philodendron sheaths, ranging in color from light tan to brown to rust, are found in tropical areas and are prevalent in Florida. Before working with philodendron leaves, soak them for about forty-five minutes first. When wet, philodendron feels like soft leather.

These photos provide examples of uses for pods, mushrooms, and philodendron sheaths.

ABOVE AND RIGHT:

Closed coil gourd with pods and beads by Linda Kincaid.

Mushroom-embellished philodendron sheath rim by the author.

(Photography by Kelly Hazel.)

LEFT:
Laraine Short's gourd embellished with berries from a Kousa Dogwood tree. She dried them, drilled holes, and used waxed linen to form a garland. *Courtesy of Laraine Short.*

CENTER:
Louise Leake's leather gourd woven with natural hemp and leather lace. The closed spokes are covered with three Philodendron sheaths. *Courtesy of Louise Leake.*

RIGHT:
Marla Helton's gourds with beads, mizuhiki, and pods. *Photography by Stuart Fabe.*

Brenda Dewald adds walnut slices in many of her pine needle basket gourds, as this rim shows. *Courtesy of Brenda Dewald.*

Natural Woods

My friends who sent me ideas for embellishments are really creative. Lynn Thomas's gourd is simple, yet so effective. She left the gourd in its natural color, cut the top, and added one vine stem. It maintains the natural beauty of the natural materials that were used in the gourd art piece. *Courtesy of Lynn Thomas.*

BOTTOM LEFT AND RIGHT:

Tanager by Bonnie Gibson. This is a great example of a carved gourd. Bonnie incorporated acrylic paints and wood carving in this gourd. She hand-carved the bird from basswood and added a Manzanita branch for the bird's perch.

Bonnie Gibson's *Butterfly Basket* is another example of a simple yet effective gourd. She used dyes and acrylic paint, root wood, a leather lace handle, and brass butterflies. The effect resulted in the gourd appearing as a type of wooden bowl with a handle.

(*Courtesy of Bonnie Gibson.*)

13

Antlers

Antlers have always been a favorite embellishment to add to gourds, especially in the West. Antlers are used for handles, bases, or just attached to the gourd or weaving to make it look interesting. Elk, deer, and moose antlers are the ones most commonly used. Betsey Sloan uses antlers in her Danish Cord. Brenda Dewald uses organic materials to weave beautiful gourd baskets. She said her inspiration for her earthy and nature-based artwork comes from everyday experiences on her Oklahoma ranch. Charlotte Durrence made a five-tiered pine needle basket gourd with a deer antler at the top and sliced walnuts as embellishments. Before coiling the pine needles, she dyed the needles black.

TOP TO BOTTOM:

Charlotte Durrence's pine needle rim with antler and walnut slices. *Photography by Derral Durrence*.

Brenda Dewald's *Papoose* features a pine needle rim embellished with an elk antler. *Courtesy of Brenda Dewald*.

LEFT:

Betsey Sloan's coiled rim with antler. *Courtesy of Betsey Sloan*.

Recycled Gourds

A recycled gourd is one that is embellished with items people throw away. In one of our patch meetings, Debbie Wilson and Betty Bloomfield taught us how to make a recycled gourd. We collected soda pop caps and tabs, assorted nails and washers, paper, string, buttons, aluminum foil, and many other things. Betty Bloomfield also used fantasy film on her gourd. We attached the items to create a pleasing design and then we painted it with thick paint and sprayed the gourd with a sealer.

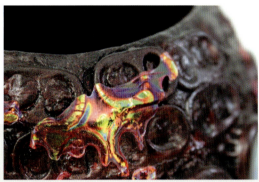

Recycled Gourd by Betty Bloomfield. Betty embellished her gourd with soda pop caps and tabs, as well as fantasy film. *Photography by Kelly Hazel.*

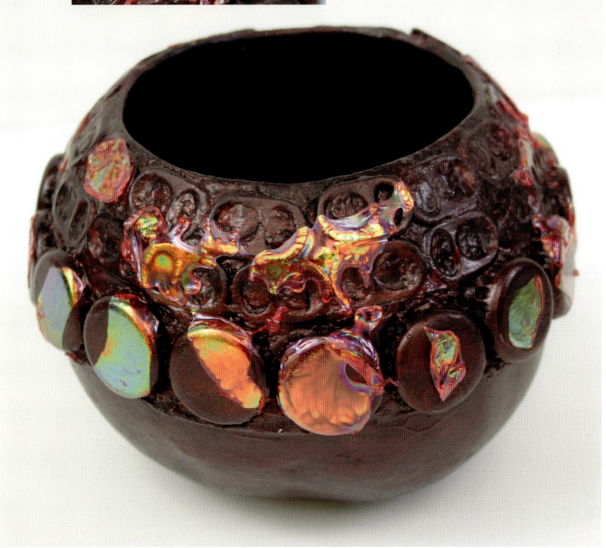

Tutorials & Patterns

Courtesy of Kristy Dial.

Tipi
by Kristy Dial

Power-carving is a wonderful technique for adding dimension to a gourd. With a little practice, you will be creating masterpieces.

MATERIALS

- A thick, dry gourd, cut and cleaned
- Dust mask and carving burrs
- Wood burner (optional)
- A Dremel or equivalent power tool (preferably with a flex-shaft and stand)
- Sandpaper – various grits
- Toothpicks or small sticks
- Acrylic paints and paintbrushes
- Ink dyes or Trans Tint dyes
- Spray varnish – Deft (Satin) or Krylon Indoor/Outdoor Varnish

INSTRUCTIONS

PREP BEFORE CARVING:

- **FIRST AND FOREMOST**: Wear a mask or respirator when cleaning the gourd and when carving.
- Do not wear loose clothing because the clothes can get caught in your tool.
- Clean the outside and inside of your gourd. Sketch the tipis or transfer your design onto the gourd using graphite or carbon paper.
- Wood-burn the outline of the tipis.

CARVING:

Carving Burrs: Steel or carbide cutters are best for working on gourds. Structured tooth carbide burrs are good for carving large areas. The wheel is great for cutting lines. The round balls are good for carving out the area of the design. Diamond bits are best for "fine-tuning" the meat of the gourd. I don't use them to remove the outer skin, as they tend to burn the gourd.

Wood-burn your design before carving, if desired. This step does seem to provide somewhat of a channel for the burr if you burn deeply. You can outline your design and then carve away all of the areas around the tipis. Carve at high to medium-high speed and put a little pressure on the bit — this helps to keep the burr from skipping.

When carving, push and pull...*push* the gourd away from you and *pull* the carver toward you. When you want to carve a straight line, look at the end point as you push the gourd away from you. Short strokes work well to help maintain a constant depth when cleaning out an area. Use the diamond bits or sanding bits to smooth out areas and refine the edges. Use sandpaper to smooth the carved areas. Deft spray varnish can be used to protect the carved area and will not yellow.

FINISHING:

- **SAND THE AREA BEHIND THE TIPIS**: If you want the color of the tipi to be lighter than the gourd, lightly sand the skin off of the tipis. Wood-burn your design on top of the tipis. Use acrylic paint to paint designs onto the tipis.
- **TOOTHPICKS**: Split them in half and paint with brown acrylic paints. Drill holes at the top of the tipis for the "poles." Put a little glue on the end of the toothpicks and insert into the gourd.
- **SMOKE**: Light a match and, holding the gourd over the match, the smoke emitted — or soot — will smoke the area around the sticks.
- **SPRAY VARNISHING**: Varnish the whole gourd with satin Deft spray. Do two to three coats.

Gourd Vase with Inset Pebbles

by Lynn Thomas

Lynn Thomas' tutorial provides the step-by-step process to create this gourd utilizing pebbles and limbs as embellishments.

This is a large gourd vase, approximately 11" high. My intention was to create a very simple and natural-looking design that featured a "stream" of inset, small multi-colored pebbles flowing around the top of the gourd.

First, I used watercolor paint to paint two curvy lines around the gourd, sort of parallel, but varying the distance between the lines to suggest the edges of a flowing stream bed with wider and narrower spots.

I used a Dremel rotary tool with a cylinder bit (#194), holding it at 90 degrees to the gourd, to cut two shallow grooves, following my watercolor lines. I was careful not to cut too deeply, for fear of "breaking through," and tried to keep the depth consistent around the gourd. I carved away the surface of the gourd between the two grooves, at the same depth as the grooves, to create the final "trench." I left the bottom of this trench rather rough so that it might hold the epoxy better. Any leftover watercolor marks on the surface of the gourd were then easily wiped off with a damp paper towel. I painted the cut edge of the top rim of the gourd with brown acrylic paint.

My goal in finishing the outside of the gourd was to let the natural markings on the gourd show through, so I applied a light tan ink (Ranger "Distress Ink" in "Vintage Photo" — this comes in an ink pad) over the whole gourd to give it a transparent caramel color and then I sprayed the gourd with several coats of clear, semi-gloss polyurethane.

Next, I painted the inside of the "trench" a dark gray/brown color, using acrylic paint. This is so that any gaps between stones would appear dark and "stream-like." Painting the trench AFTER the gourd had been finished with polyurethane made it easy to wipe off any slip-ups where paint ended up on the surface of the gourd rather than in the trench!

In order to adhere the small pebbles to the inside of the trench, I used a two-part epoxy. I mixed small amounts of epoxy as I went, since it hardens up quickly. I would apply some epoxy to a small section of the carved-out "trench" and then place small river pebbles into the epoxy. I placed the pebbles as close together as I could, trying to fill small gaps with small pebbles. I continued around the gourd, doing one small section at a time. When the epoxy hardened and the stones were set, the gourd was finished. Places where the transparent epoxy showed between or on the sides of the pebbles looked "wet," only enhancing the effect.

TOP:

Gourd vase with inset pebbles by Lynn Thomas.
Courtesy of Lynn Thomas.

Antler Bowl with Horse Hair

BY KAREN HUNT-BROWN

I really enjoy weaving with different materials and trying different embellishments to add to my artwork. When I use antlers in my weaving, it's always a marriage between the gourd and the antler(s). I find that some gourds are better suited for two or more antlers while others only need one to complement the piece. This gourd was acquired at the Kentucky Gourd Show for its size and weight. I wanted one that would stand on its own with the added weight, and this gourd fit the bill. I then pulled out my box of antlers and played with them all until I found the one that looked best with the gourd. A lot of my antler pieces have asymmetrical openings, and I love the look and the way the whole piece flows together — these odd openings just lend themselves well to interesting weavings.

I laid out the opening for the piece and penciled it in. I then cut, cleaned, and sanded (inside and out) the gourd, and dyed the inside with leather dye while on the outside I used dark walnut wood stain by Minwax.

I sealed the piece with Minwax oil satin finish and drilled the holes for the weaving, half-an-inch down and half-an-inch apart. I like the holes to be this close together as I usually only do single-stitch work.

When I had the gourd ready for weaving, I had to select the material I would use and that turned out to be something different than my usual pine needle. The banana-skinned rope I had looked well with the gourd and the antler. I love dyed and natural pine needles for weaving, but this piece just looked so much better with the rope. I never really liked to see the holes in my weavings, so I learned how to cover them up with the first row and then continue on with the successive rows. I had gotten three rounds on, was past the rim and about to add the antler, when I had to figure out just how the weaving was going to intertwine with the horn. This part had me stuck for a week, and I finally just kept playing with the remaining rope till it worked. I finished the weaving and then started the embellishment.

I really loved the look of the stem the gourd had, but it was far too damaged to keep, so I replaced it with a horse hair tassel. I found this piece to be finished at this point as I tried to add more, but nothing really looked right, so I left it alone. Sometimes simpler is better.

TOP:

Courtesy of Karen Hunt-Brown.

Ammonite Gourd

BY LYNN THOMAS

"From the Sea: I love embellishments from the sea. I have so many shells and items found along the shores that they take up an entire shelf in my studio. I even like to wood-burn and paint shells on gourds. Lynn Thomas wrote a tutorial for using an ammonite as an embellishment. Her rim is carved and the ammonite helped to create the design. Ammonites are the most widely known fossils. They are an extinct group of marine invertebrate animals. You can purchase ammonites from Arizona Gourds."

This vase, about 10-inch high, features an inset ammonite fossil. This is part of a rim design that also includes a bit of carving. I placed the ammonite on the surface of the gourd in the exact place I wanted it to be inset and traced around it with a pencil. I examined the back of the ammonite to see where it was thickest and where it tapered toward the edges. I did this to get some idea of how much of the gourd would have to be cut away to inset the ammonite deeply into its surface. Although it wouldn't matter if part of the gourd had to be entirely cut out in order for the thick ammonite to be deeply inset, I also needed to leave enough of the gourd beneath the ammonite in order to glue it firmly in place.

I marked places on the gourd where I thought I'd have to carve deeply to accommodate the thickest part of the ammonite and then started carving away these areas, using a Dremel rotary tool with a ball-tip burr. I had the ammonite with me at the work bench so that I could repeatedly fit the ammonite into my carved area — I'd make note of where it did and didn't lay perfectly into its spot on the gourd. Sure enough, I had to carve totally through a certain spot in the gourd in order to accommodate the thickest part of the ammonite, but toward the edges there was enough of the gourd surface to glue it. When I knew that the ammonite could be inset perfectly into its spot on the gourd, I put it aside and finished the rest of the gourd. I saved the actual gluing in of the ammonite until the very end.

With a pencil, I drew the lines that would be carved around the rim of the gourd and around the ammonite. Between the lines, using the cylinder tip on the Dremel, I carved the surface of the gourd in a design pattern that would suggest the segments in the ammonite. I also carved a thin line around the very top of the gourd using a small ball-tip burr. I then applied Fiebing's mahogany leather dye to the entire outside of the gourd. Areas where the surface of the gourd had been carved away absorbed more dye and came out looking darker. After the dye had dried, I sprayed the gourd with a light coat of clear, semi-gloss polyurethane. When that dried, I went back to the carving bench and used a medium-sized ball-tip burr in my Dremel to carve out the two lines that frame this rim design. I carved them after the gourd had been dyed, so that these lines, un-dyed, would reveal the gourd's natural color and produce a nice contrast effect.

I then sprayed the gourd with several additional coats of clear, semi-gloss polyurethane. Finally, I used a two-part epoxy to adhere the ammonite to its carved-out spot on the gourd.

TOP:

Courtesy of Lynn Thomas.

Gourds with Wire Shapes

BEGINNER LEVEL

BY ANGIE WAGNER

Photos in this section courtesy of Angie Wagner

Please read through the entire pattern before starting. Directions are written from the right-hand point of view.

RECOMMENDED TOOLS:

- Protective Dust Mask
- Plastic Scrubbers/Scraping Tool/Scouring Pad
- Eversand Pads #1400 & #1401
- Basket Shear (heavy-duty, sharp scissors)
- Carving Knife
- 1/2" Rubber Tipped Clamps
- Pointed Awl with graduated metal shank/Drill

TOP TO BOTTOM:

Angie Wagner's *Gourds with Wire Shapes* baskets and the material she used.

MATERIALS

- Tapestry or Large Eye Needle
- Dried, cleaned, and cut Hard-shell Bottle Gourd (See the Cleaning & Cutting Sections)
- Pine Needles, Philodendron Sheaths, Wool Roving, Braided Seagrass, Textured Yarn, Leather Lacing, or other materials to embellish the top of the gourd
- Wire Shape
- 4-ply Waxed Linen — approximately 8-10 times the diameter of your gourd opening
- Various small beads
- Beeswax & Double Boiler

INSTRUCTIONS

Breathing gourd dust and mold spores can be harmful to your health so be sure to wear protective gear over your mouth and nose while cleaning, cutting, and sanding gourds. Keeping the gourd wet while cleaning and cutting can reduce the risk, but it is better to be protected at all times while preparing gourds.

The methods explained in this pattern are what work well for me. You may find different information from other sources. I have tried to be as thorough as possible, but due to differences in skills, materials, tools, and conditions I cannot offer a guarantee nor accept any liability for loss, injury or damage as a result of using the information in this pattern.

As stated at the beginning of the project, please read through the entire pattern before starting.

CLEANING THE OUTSIDE OF THE GOURD:

Place the gourd in warm water for fifteen minutes; keep rotating the gourd so all sides are exposed to the water. Begin scrubbing the outer layers of epidermis, mold, and dirt with a plastic or copper scrubber. Do not push hard on the gourd while scrubbing, as there may be a weak spot or, if the gourd shell is thin, you could push right through into the shell. You may want to alternate scrubbing and soaking if the gourd has a waxy outer layer. When the worst has been cleaned off, switch to a finer scrubbing pad until the gourd is smooth and clean. Be careful to not scratch the surface of the gourd.

The gourd may have stains left on the surface by the mold (gourds dry from the inside out and mold collects on the surface as the moisture reaches the outer epidermis layers). Personally, I believe that these color variations enhance the appearance of the finished gourd. If you do not agree and wish to have a gourd that is more uniform in color, you may want to use bleach or a hydrogen peroxide bath. If you use BLEACH to remove stains, after cleaning with water, be sure to rinse with vinegar and water to counteract the negative effects of bleach on the gourd fibers. If you use HYDROGEN PEROXIDE, work outside and be sure to protect yourself from fumes. Boil a pot of hydrogen peroxide and add the gourds to the pot, rotating them for complete coverage. When the outer gunk and dirt is falling off, carefully remove the gourds and rinse with water. Scrub as needed. The gourds should have a more golden color with a reduction in the appearance of stains.

Cutting the Gourd — Part One:

While the gourd is still wet, use the Basket Shear to cut the top off of the gourd. You can use a pencil to draw a guideline. Hold the Basket Shear vertically so that you are using just the tips to cut into the gourd. Do not try to dig too deeply into the gourd the first time around. Gourd shell thickness varies on each gourd. If you have a thin gourd, once around may be enough; if the gourd has a thicker shell, you may need to re-cut several times. The top of the gourd can be flipped upside-down and used for a vase.

Cleaning the Inside of the Gourd:

You will need to shake out any loose material and seeds. Put the gourd back in warm water to thoroughly soak the inside. Use a scraping tool (loops of flat metal make great scraping tools, check pottery tools for possibilities), file, serrated spoon, etc. to clean the inside. Remove as much of the white material from the inside as possible in order to reveal the clean, suede-like inner shell.

Cutting the Gourd — Part Two:

When you have removed as much as possible from scraping, trim the opening to the desired shape and size with a carving knife. The knife will cut through the gourd a little easier while it is wet. Be careful to cut slowly and carefully. It is possible to split the gourd down the growth lines. If you need to create holes around the top of the gourd (needed for this pattern), use a very sharp awl with a graduated tip. With a twisting motion, insert the awl approximately 1/4" - 3/8" from the top. Slowly push the awl into the gourd. Turn the gourd and place a hole on the opposite side. Split the distance between the holes with a new hole. Continue to split the distance between the holes with a new hole until you have placed holes all around the gourd. Keep the holes approximately 1/4" - 1/2" apart. You can use a soft tape measure and mark the distance with a pencil to be exact — OR drill holes in your DRY gourd with a drill. Putting in the holes can also be done after the gourd has been bees-waxed or sealed. Set the gourd aside to dry.

Note: Make sure the gourd is completely dry before going on to the next step. Use the Eversand® pad or sandpaper to sand the inside of the gourd to remove any remaining white material. Sand until the inside is smooth; also sand any jagged edges around the top.

Dyeing Gourds:

If you wish to dye the gourd, do so at this point. Leather dyes and inks can be brushed or wiped onto the inside and outside of the gourd. They can be layered. You can also use fiber dyes (also used for basket reed). Simply immerse the gourd in a dye bath until it reaches the color you like. Let the gourd dry thoroughly before treating the gourd with beeswax. *Note: If you want to sign your name with an ink pen. you must do it before adding the beeswax. You can use a wood-burning tool at any time.*

Treating the Gourd with Beeswax: You need to place the gourds into a preheated oven at 175 degrees for 10 – 15 minutes in order to ensure the wax will penetrate the pores of the gourds. Gourds are flammable — do NOT leave the kitchen. Slowly melt the beeswax in a double boiler. Wax is very flammable — do NOT walk away from the melting wax. Once the wax is melted, place the warm gourd into the wax pot. Rotate the gourd with tongs until the entire gourd is covered, inside and outside. Drain excess wax and place on paper towel to cool. This will strengthen and semi-waterproof the gourd and give it a nice smell. A heavy coat of beeswax on the inside will waterproof the gourd.

Design Your Rim:

Lay your coiling material onto the raw edge of the gourd and clamp in place with rubber-tipped clamps. The softer the material, the easier it is to work with — so beginners might want to try yarn or wool roving at first. Depending on the materials you are using, you can tuck the ends under the coil or cross them in the front. The wool roving was tucked under the coil and around the wire bar. If your wire shape has edges that turn down, straighten them with a pair of needle-nose pliers so the bar is straight across. You can then curve the bar to the shape of your gourd opening. Remove just the clamps at the back of your gourd and tuck the bar of the wire under your coiling material.

TOP:
Coiling material on the raw edge of the gourd and clamped in place with rubber-tipped clamps.

BOTTOM LEFT AND RIGHT:
Examples of two rims: the first has a small seagrass rim, the other a braided flat seagrass rim.

BEGINNING THE LASHING WITH WAXED LINEN:

If wax or sealer has accumulated in the holes, carefully open the holes with an awl. Thread your needle with (8-9 times the diameter of the opening) the waxed linen. If you want to have a beaded tail, start with the tail to the outside (approx. 6" through the hole.) Bring the needle through the "front" hole to the inside of the gourd and then up and over the rim of your gourd and whatever coiling material you have decided to use. Insert the needle into the next hole to the right (when looking at the front of your gourd). If you do not want a beaded tail, leave a tail (2-3 inches) tucked under the coiling material. You will continue bringing the waxed linen over the rim of the gourd and inserting the needle into the next hole to the right all the way around the gourd rim. You want to pull the waxed linen tight, but not so hard that you cut into the gourd. Hold your current lash in place while you insert the needle into the next hole so they do not loosen. When you get to the wire shape, you want to make sure that you have the bar secured and completely hidden under the coiling material. Your waxed linen thread will go over the bar and secure the wire in place. You may want to lash through the wire shape as well, depending on the shape.

TOP AND BOTTOM:

The lashing is done using waxed linen thread.

 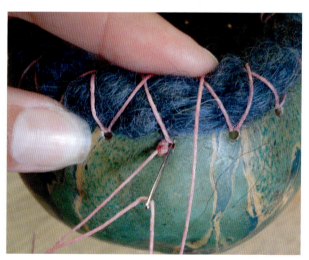

TOP: LEFT AND RIGHT

Tuck the bar of the wire embellishment under your coiling material.

The wax linen will hold the rim and wire shapes in place.

CENTER: LEFT AND RIGHT

Continue lashing the rim around the gourd.

Keep the lashing tight as you go around the rim.

BOTTOM: LEFT AND RIGHT

You will be going back around the rim again to make an "x" at each hole.

This is the last time.

Adding the Beads:

Now bring the needle, working from the inside of the gourd, one hole to the right (or left) and through to the outside. You will most likely have to remove the needle to add small beads. Twirl the end of the waxed linen to create a point. Add beads (groups of three are pleasing to the eye, but it will depend on the space between the holes and the size of your beads) and bring the waxed linen to the inside, one hole to the right (or left). You can also add beads on the inside of the gourd if you like. Continue until you reach the start. If you wish, continue around again to completely fill the top with beads (you may have to reverse direction depending on the number of holes). If you are finished, loop the needle through the closest stitch on the inside of the gourd. Make a small knot and bring the thread through the coiling, cut, and tuck end (if you are not doing the beaded tails) or bring tail out through the "front" hole (to make another beaded tail) and tie a knot just to the outside of the hole to keep everything tight. You can add one or more 8" - 10" piece/s of waxed linen at the spot of your tail. Knot around or through your first knotted tail to hold in place. Add beads to your liking, stagger ends, knot ends of thread, or trim and fray ends of the thread by pulling through fingernails or across a scissor blade. I used tiny buttons as beads on the gourd with the heart wire. I found them in the button section of a fabric store. HAPPY WEAVING!

ABOVE AND RIGHT:

Getting ready to add beads.

Adding beads under the rim.

GALLERY

I entered in the South Carolina State Fair where this gourd won a Patron Award. The gourd has carving, woodburning, inset dichroic glass cabochons, a dreamcatcher, a philodendron sheath rim, and starfish.

Siren by Marianne Barnes. Full and close-up views show the dreamcatcher with a starfish embellishment. *Photography by Kelly Hazel.*

This image depicts two gourds that have a look of raku pottery. I took this class from Bonnie Gibson several years ago in Georgia. To achieve the raku effect, black glue and sand are mixed together and applied to the gourd. The colors come from Lumiere sprays and Pearl Ex powders. A dragonfly embellishment was added to complete the gourd.

Patricia Ramsey provided the carved gourd with a starfish for a fundraiser at the Cherokee Gourd Gathering. I was the thrilled recipient of the gourd and I am sharing it here with Patricia's permission.

TOP:
Raku bowls by Marianne Barnes. *Photography by Kelly Hazel.*

LEFT AND RIGHT:
Courtesy of Patricia Ramsey.

Courtesy of Louise Leake.

Louise Leake created this gourd with a silk dye effect that looks like the ocean. This is an excellent example of how the embellishments complement the gourd. Here is Louise's description of the gourd: "The silk dyed gourd is finished with a Gretchen rim, which I wanted to embellish with a marine theme since the design on the gourd reminded me of fish. Using a 3/4" button, I sewed two strands of waxed linen from the front near the fish design, through the rim, around the reeds, and then back through the other hole in the button. After securing the button to the rim with a square knot, I attached shells to each of the threads with a knot at the end of the threads. Next, I used a shell that has a conical shape and glued it to the button, allowing the shelled threads to fall between the shell and the button. I filled in any space between the shell and the gourd with dried moss, which looks like seaweed, to complete the project."

Marla Helton and Stu Fabe create exquisite gourds. Marla loves to use embellishments that appear to be metal, but are actually made of air-dried clay, stamped with metallic rub-on. Marla also uses wire, especially copper. Stu's coiling with Danish cording is absolutely perfect. He uses small embellishments that give just a hint of excitement. He uses the beautiful earthy colors of the Danish cording to contrast the color of the gourd. Here you can see a variety of embellishments.

Wire and embossed clay embellishments by Marla Helton and Stuart Fabe. *Photography by Stuart Fabe.*

Simple Pleasures looks as though the gourd has a collar. The rim is Danish Cord and the embellishments are embossed metal and beads. *Sedona Sunset* has a rim made of coiled horsehair. The embellishment in the front is metal that has been embossed. *The Journey* has a Danish cord rim and the embellishments are made of metal and copper wire. These gourds were created by Marla Helton with photography by Stuart Fabe.

TOP LEFT:

Bead and metal embellishment. *Photography by Stuart Fabe.*

BOTTOM LEFT AND RIGHT:

Stu Fabe is an expert coiler using Danish cord. He uses small accent embellishments.

Stu Fabe's embellished this gourd with flailed ends of the Danish.

(Photography by Stuart Fabe.)

Kristy Dial was one of the first gourd artists who started using hammered copper shards. Kristy cuts the copper into the desired shapes and hammers the copper to create the designs in the copper shard.

I prefer to weave and wood-burn on gourds, but this piece called for an embellishment of clay. The wood-burned magnolia on the gourd was inspiration for the clay magnolias. Our local patch has been fortunate to have Peggy Ash as a member. Peggy works with all types of clay: air-dry clays, polymer clays, Apoxie® Sculpt, and many more. Both myself and my granddaughter enjoy working with clay after a class with Peggy.

TOP LEFT AND RIGHT:

Kristie Dial's hammered copper shards. *Courtesy of Kristy Dial.*

BOTTOM LEFT AND RIGHT:

Flower embellishment on inside of gourd.

Magnolia by Marianne Barnes has a flower on top as an embellishment.

(Photography by Kelly Hazel.)

Professional gourd artist Bonnie Gibson stated: "One of my primary goals is to help lift gourds out of the realm of 'crafts' and into greater acceptance as fine art. To that end, I enjoy manipulating gourds in new ways, inviting the viewer to interpret them as something more while retaining their natural essence." Here, embellishments include the sculpted lizard sculpture (Apoxie® Sculpt), brass butterflies, and a cholla cactus skeleton.

Courtesy of Bonnie Gibson.

Peggy Ash creates gourd and clay figures. In the lidded gourd bowl, Quickwood® was used. Quickwood is a polymer compound for instant wood repair. It is easy to use, molds like clay, and it dries like wood in thirty minutes. It also bonds to gourds. Peggy uses it when teaching classes because it dries quickly. She taught this gourd project at the annual Mountain Gourd Gathering in Cedar Mountain, North Carolina. She showed participants how to form the strawberries and leaves and, using clay tools, how to make the berries and leaves look realistic. Peggy recommends using white glue to adhere the Quickwood to the gourd to ensure the stability of the embellishment.

TOP LEFT AND RIGHT:

Berry bowl by Peggy Ash.

Peggy Ash picks out the perfect shape for a bowl and uses Quikwood for making the leaves and berries.

(Photography by Kelly Hazel.)

BOTTOM LEFT AND RIGHT:

Painting the leaves on the berry bowl.

Finished berry bowl by Peggy Ash.

(Photography by Kelly Hazel.)

Dragonfly Bowl by Betsey Sloan. Betsey added a dragonfly to her gourd as an embellishment using black Apoxie® Sculpt for the body. The wings are seed pods from a maple tree. The wings were dusted with Pearl-Ex powders and then coated with 3-D lacquer to strengthen them.

Photography by Kelly Hazel.

Rose Vase with wooden lid and base by Paul Morris. Paul works with both wood and gourds, and has created gourd lids that swing open and close. A wood base, embellished with copper, was added to the bottom of this gourd.

Photography by Kelly Hazel.

Linda Kincaid is a member of the South Carolina Gourd Society and has taught at the annual Ghost Creek Gourd Fest and the Mountain Gourd Gathering. An accomplished wood-burner, Linda has added a special embellishments to her wood-burned gourds. To this one, she added a lid and a base. The lid is decorated with geometric wood shapes.

TOP LEFT AND RIGHT:

Linda Kincaid's gourd embellishment with pieces of geometric wood.

Finished gourd by Linda Kincaid.

(Photography by Kelly Hazel.)

Betsey Sloan also made a recycled gourd. The gourd technique is called Old World. The base was painted with acrylic black paint. Various pieces of lace were glued on and more black paint applied. The squiggles are simply cordage that Betsey had in the studio. She glued them on and painted them black. The overall gourd was dabbed with various acrylic colors: gold, turquoise, copper, and some red.

Recycled Bowl by Betsey Sloan.
Photography by Kelly Hazel.

Masks

Masks by Debbie Wilson. The mask was dyed and then embellished with carving. Debbie's carving adds a great deal of interest to the mask. *Photography by Kelly Hazel.*

Gourd masks lend themselves well for the use of embellishments. Since I weave, I add woven areas on masks I create; recently, I wove a nose and mouth with small round reed on a mask. Some embellishments that can be added to masks are: porcupine quills, feathers, leather, horse hair, carved bone tusks, bone beads, cones, inlayed cabochons, wood, as well as many other materials.

Making a Mask

Debbie Wilson, a carver, begins her masks by staining them. She carves with small round and straight bits. Dental bits work great for this type of detailed carving. The green leaf mask was dyed with Trans Tint® dyes. She made a border of dark green and blue and the rest was dyed with yellow and green. She carved shapes in the dark green border and then carved leaves vertically down the center. Debbie also carved lines around the eyes and then did some shading on the mask.

You can use strands from the inside of kudzu, or seagrass, around the top of the mask for hair. The brown mask with circles was dyed with brown, black, and yellow Trans Tint and sanded with #400 grit wet dry sandpaper, especially where the brown is very dark. It was then coated with fixative. She used Quickwood for the teeth. She also drilled holes on the sides of the mask and attached beads with waxed linen thread. She then sprayed it with a clear acrylic sealer.

On the black-brown mask, Debbie carved small lines and circles around the black area that looks like bubbles. She added brown hair and wire as embellishments. The mouth is another gourd piece that has been attached with wire through holes drilled out around that area.

While Debbie carved circles and lines on her mask, there are other, different designs out there that can be used. Don't be afraid to try new things and don't be afraid to carve on your gourds. You can really use any shape and dye and then just carve lines, circles, and more. When Debbie taught the mask class at our patch meeting, she said to just have fun!

Photography by Kelly Hazel.

TOP to BOTTOM:

Full and close-up views of mask by Debbie Wilson. Debbie adds beads and waxed linen thread to the mask for hair. *Photography by Kelly Hazel.*

TOP TO BOTTOM:

In this mask by Debbie Wilson, wire and waxed linen was added at the top, as well as a stitched gourd mouth. *Photography by Kelly Hazel.*

Gallery of Mask

BY DON WEEKE

Don Weeke's gourd art is well known. Form and texture are important elements of his art. In his masks, he uses embellishments such as dowels, acorn caps, wood, waxed linen, date palm, antlers, palm fronds, plywood and fiber board, washers, nails, and raffia. Enjoy this gallery of masks courtesy of Don Weeke.

TOP TO BOTTOM:

4 Directions. 17" x 17" x 3-1/2". Materials are gourd, paint, wood, and dowels.

Acorn Spirit. 13" x 13" x 2-1/2". Materials are acorn caps, gourd, paint, dowels, and waxed linen.

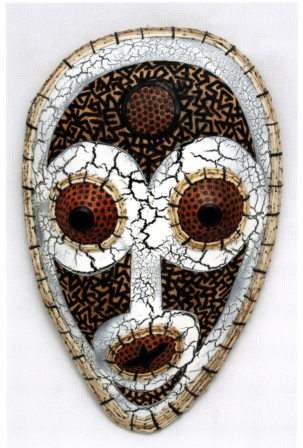

CLOCKWISE:

Cheeks & Eyebrows. 20-1/2" x 8-1/2" x 2-1/2". Materials are gourd, paint, and date palm frond. Techniques: pyrography and couching.

Coded Textures. 17" x 11" x 3-1/2". Materials are gourd, paint, date palm frond. Techniques: pyrography and couching.

Deer Spirit. 22" x 10-1/2" x 9". Materials are gourd, paint, deer antler, and raffia.

LEFT:

Diablo. 20" x 14" x 4-1/2". Materials are gourd and paint.

CENTER:

Dot Punker. 12-1/2" x 12-1/2" x 2". Materials are gourd, paint, and fiber board.

RIGHT:

Dot Warrior. 23" x 14" x 5". Materials are gourd, paint plywood. Technique is pyrography.

LEFT:

Double Speak. 19" x 13-1/2" x 2-1/2". Materials are gourd, acorn caps, dowels, and king palm frond. Techniques: pyrography and weaving.

CENTER:

Dot Seer. 20" x 13-1/2" x 2-1/2". Materials are gourd, paint, date palm frond.

RIGHT:

Metal Man. 23" x 13" x 4-1/2". Materials include rivets, washers, and paint.

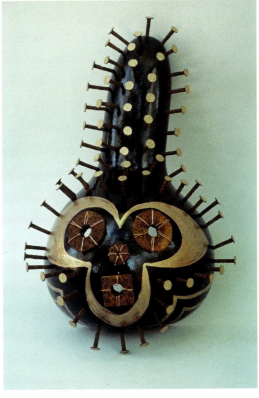

LEFT:

Mudhead. 16-1/2" x 10" x 5". Materials are gourd, raffia, paint.

CENTER:

Nailed. 12" x 7-1/2" x3". Materials are gourd, nails, and washers.

RIGHT:

Shaman's Wink. 15-1/2" x 15" x 5". Materials are gourd, antler, raffia, and paint. Technique is pyrography.

LEFT:

White Nose. 19" x 15" x 4". Materials are gourd, paint, and wood dowels.

CENTER:

Pinocchio Tells a Whopper. 22" x 11" x 10". Materials are gourd and paint.

RIGHT:

Zigzag. 14" x 15" x 3". Materials are gourd, paint, waxed linen.

GALLERY

My good friend and a member of the Palmetto Gourd Patch, Ruth Clinkingbeard, passed away recently. She was a wonderful gourd artist. Ruth was creative and was willing to try any new technique. Her family shared her gourds with the patch and allowed me to use some in this book. We miss Ruth and her happy attitude and excitement she brought to the members of the patch. Ruth's mask was embellished with feathers, yarn, beads, and earrings.

Mask by Ruth Clinkingbeard. This is a memorial to her. *Photography by Kelly Hazel.*

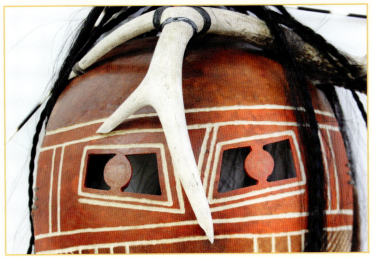

Wayne Anderson is a member of our local patch. He is new to gourds, but has become an accomplished gourd artist. Wayne chose to carve his masks after a class with Debbie Wilson.

LEFT TOP TO BOTTOM:

Mask by Wayne Anderson. Embellishments include feathers, antler, horsehair, and porcupine quills. *Photography by Kelly Hazel.*

RIGHT TOP TO BOTTOM:

Gourd pieces were attached with leather to form the ears of the mask.

Wayne added a mouth by cutting out a small gourd piece and gluing it onto the mask.

(Photography by Kelly Hazel.)

Dr. Linda Lake is an exceptional chip-carver. She used the chip-carving technique on this mask as an embellishment. She also used acrylics, raffia, feathers, and beading.

My Mask of Many Colors by Dr. Linda Lake. 11" x 10". *Courtesy of Dr. Linda Lake.*

Ruth Gedroic created this mask using natural materials for embellishments: longleaf pine, Spanish moss, shells, feathers, pods, and parts of palm. The eyes are shells and the hair is longleaf pine needles and moss.

Courtesy of Ruth Gedroic.

Marla Helton selected some unusual materials as embellishments on her masks. Clockwise: The yellow mask has wire, powdered pigment on beads, colored wire for the hair, puff painters for the necklace, beads, palm inflorescence for the nose, and wood-burning around the eyes, all on a gourd that was painted yellow. The large red mask, stained a reddish color, has wire, old hardware, palm inflorescence, beads, and metal washers. The orange mask was stained and has unfurled Danish cord for the hair, feathers, beads, suede, a washer, a deer bone for the nose, and wire. You might call these recycled masks.

TOP LEFT AND RIGHT:

Yellow Mask by Marla Helton.

Large Red Mask by Marla Helton.

(Photography by Stuart Fabe.)

BOTTOM RIGHT:

The Orange Mask by Marla Helton. Photography by Stuart Fabe.

Bonnie Gibson's *Wild Brothers Mask* uses a round gourd as a base. The embellishments are turkey, macaw, pheasant feathers, horsehair, brass cones, antlers, turquoise, and leather. The cones are useful in keeping the horsehair neat and attaching them to the gourd.

Wild Brothers Mask – approx. 24" wide. *Courtesy of Bonnie Gibson.*

Jack Thorpe from Long Beach, California, created *Tribal Bear* and *Coyote*. The gourds were cut, painted, wood-burned, and embellished with extra pieces of gourd and the addition of raffia and beads. Jack used a pin to shred the raffia to make it look like hair. Jack uses very few embellishments, but they are so effective in making the gourd art complete.

LEFT AND RIGHT:

Tribal Bear by Jack Thorpe.

Coyote by Jack Thorpe.

(*Courtesy of Jack Thorpe.*)

Iris Durand has made several gourd masks using embellishments. Gourds are stained and the designs carved. The first mask was embellished with horsehair and raffia. She added long bone beads at the ear area and small beads in the raffia. In both masks, Iris cut out the eye area and added another piece of gourd underneath. The extra piece has a metal stud as an eye. Both gourds also have a separate piece of a gourd as a mouth. The smaller gourd mask has wooden washer beads and palm stems for hair.

TOP LEFT AND RIGHT:

Gourd masks by Iris Durand. *Photography by Kelly Hazel.*

BOTTOM RIGHT

Iris wrapped the horsehair in bunches and glued them in pre-drilled holes on back of the masks. *Photography by Kelly Hazel.*

LEFT AND RIGHT:

Lee used feathers and horsehair for hair.

A hanging shell earring on Lee's mask.

(Photography by Kelly Hazel.)

Lee Tuttle is in the Palmetto Gourd Patch and she made this gourd using raffia, beads, and feathers. She carved the eyebrows and eyes, as well as did some carving on the cheek. The dye on the masks and the embellishments give it a natural look.

TOP LEFT:

Photography by Kelly Hazel.

RIGHT; TOP TO BOTTOM:

The horsehair is glued to Lee's mask.

Lee embellished raffia with beads.

(Photography by Kelly Hazel.)

Dolls and Whimsical Gourds

Have fun with your gourd art! These whimsical gourds are proof you can have fun. Gourd dolls can be created in many different ways. My gourd doll is titled *Mommy Dearest*, and she is made from a very large kettle gourd. The gourd was cut, cleaned, and dyed. Another small gourd was inserted in the top for a head. Banana gourds were cut in half and attached for the childrens' bodies. The heads are small jewelry gourds. Some carving and attaching wire and beads completed the gourd doll. I think the doll has a "robot" look.

CLOCKWISE:

Mommy Dearest by Marianne Barnes.

Close-up of baby embellishment in author's gourd.

The head of *Mommy Dearest* shows the bead embellishments.

(Photography by Kelly Hazel.)

Wild Women of Gourdonia

The book, *Wild Women of Gourdonia*, came from the imaginations of Marla Helton and Stu Fabe. From Stu's website, www.stuartfabe.net, he states: "Whimsical stories in the book will make you smile, and their simple messages about celebrating each other and respecting the land remind us of what is truly important in life." You can order the book at Stu's website. Here are a few examples of the "Wild Women" pins made from gourd pieces, wire, beads, feathers, and various other embellishments.

Wild Women of Gourdonia by Marla Helton and Stu Fabe.

LEFT TO RIGHT:

Juanita Pill by Marla Helton.

Ginger by Marla Helton.

Little Mama by Stu Fabe.

Photography of pins by Stuart Fabe.

TOP: LEFT TO RIGHT

Mattie by Stu Fabe.

Phoebe by Marla Helton.

Pix by Stu Fabe.

BOTTOM: LEFT TO RIGHT

Celeste by Marla Helton.

Willi Shakespearia by Stu Fabe.

Tutorials & Patterns

Wild Woman Pin

This pattern was designed by Marla Helton. It is very basic because Marla desires to inspire you to use your imagination. She still teaches Wild Women pins at workshops, conventions, and retreats. You can make a large Wild Woman to use as a wall-hanging.

MATERIALS

- 1/4- to 1/2-inch thick gourd pieces for head and body cleaned, dyed, and sealed
- Assorted wire – mostly twenty and eighteen gauges and sixteen gauge for neck wires
- Beads, feathers, suede, and various embellishments (use your imagination)
- Waxed linen thread (2- to 4-ply)
- Glue gun or quick-setting glue

Preparing the Pieces:

Cut a piece of cleaned gourd the desired shape for the body. Cut a head to complement the size and shape of the body. When cutting the pieces, keep in mind that your gourd needs to be thick enough to secure the wires into the neck, arms, and legs. Sand the sides and back of the gourd with medium grit sandpaper (about 150 grit). Spray the back and sides with black spray paint and allow them to dry. Apply the color of your choice to the front and seal. I usually use leather dye and Design Master spray and seal with a good sealer. *Note: You may want to experiment with different designs and ideas that you want to use on your Wild Woman on paper before applying them to the gourd.*

Body:

Using your imagination, you can use just about any embellishment: beads, wire, feathers, buttons — the list is limited only by your imagination. To attach various pieces, drill two holes fairly close together. Take your waxed linen thread and form a "U" with the base of the U going over the item you want to attach. Take the two ends of the U and put them through the two holes so that they come out the back of the gourd. Tie a square knot to secure. It is usually best to attach with waxed linen because it gives a more secure hold, but some things need to be glued.

For the legs and arms you will need to drill holes at the top and bottom of the body to represent where you want them to be placed. Put a wire through the hole and bring it back towards the wire and wrap a couple of times around the wire to secure. You can put beads and/or fiber to create interesting arms, legs, knees, feet, etc.

Note: The head and the body should be flat at the point that they will be attached, because you will be using two wires to go into the bottom of the head and top of the body to form the neck.

Head:

Decide what you want to use to represent the eyes, nose, and mouth and attach them with waxed linen thread. You can add earrings and other embellishments as desired. There are several ways to create hair. You can drill holes through the top of the gourd head and insert wires that you insert like a U. These can be twisted and beads can be added. You can also use mizuhiki, wrapping it around a toothpick to create ringlets. Again, use your imagination.

Neck:

When the head and body are complete, it's time to attach the head to the body. Drill two holes in the bottom of the head and two holes that correspond in the top of the body. Using 16-gauge wire, gently slip the wires into the head and make certain they fit well. Pull the wires out and put a spot of glue on them and reinsert them. Let the glue dry.

Pin:

The last step is to attach a pin back with Quick glue. You may want to give the back one last spray of black paint to give it a more finished look. Be careful not to let the paint get on the front.

GALLERY

Betsey Sloan's gourd, *Effigy,* appears to be a piece of pottery. She used clay to add embellishments. Paint and beads gave this gourd an African fetish touch.

Photography by Kelly Hazel.

Betty Bloomfield created the Bronze Cat using a Chinese bottle gourd and Quickwood embellishments. The tail, feet, ears, nose, cheeks, and eyes were all made with the Quickwood. She then added wire whiskers and a collar made from upholstery gimp and beads. The cat was painted and then Betty used bronze antiquing.

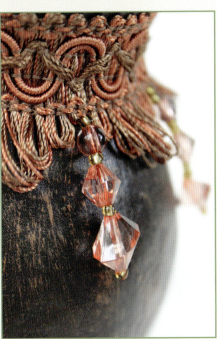

TOP LEFT AND RIGHT, BOTTOM RIGHT:

Betty Bloomfield's cat is embellished with clay, wire, and upholstery material. *Photography by Kelly Hazel.*

BOTTOM LEFT:

Elephant Bowl by Betty Bloomfield. She used Apoxie Sculpt to form the nose, ears, feet, tusks, and eyes. *Photography by Kelly Hazel.*

Patty Snearly created several whimsical fish from gourds. Holes were drilled in a larger gourd to create a light. This small fish was a banana gourd that was wood-burned. Color was added afterwards. The hook was an interesting embellishment. Other embellishments, including metal, wire, and gourd pieces, helped make this whimsical gourd look like the "real thing." Patty also added a snap swivel, which is used between your fishing line and the leader.

CLOCKWISE:

Fish by Patty Snearly. Fishing line hook, wire, and pieces of gourd for the fins were used for embellishments. *Photography by Kelly Hazel.*

Don Weeke's gourds are so much fun. What do you think this could be? If I had five people give me an answer, I would probably have five different ones. My husband said it looked like a sewing basket. The embellishments are pine needles and pine cones. Don cut the gourd and put the feet on it, painted it, and coiled the top, leaving the ends on the needles.

Pine Urn by Don Weeke. *Courtesy of Don Weeke.*

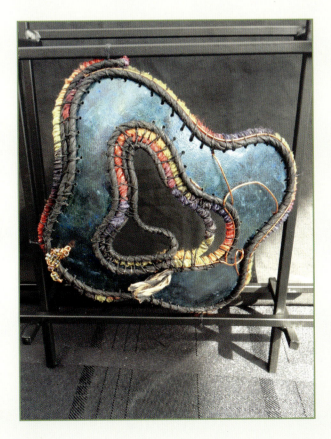

Deborah Mann created this sculptured gourd piece in a class taught by Marla Helton. The embellishments are dyed paper rush, waxed linen thread, and beads. The bright color of the rush and the metallic color of the gourd shard works together to make the gourd art look complete. The iron base also serves as an embellishment.

Marla teaches many classes, especially in the East. On her website, www.serendipitygourdart.com, she says: "I travel around the country to conventions, retreats and workshops teaching others how to create using gourds, pottery and weaving. Teaching others to expand their own imagination is very rewarding to me. Most classes that I teach provide the basic knowledge to inspire my students to pursue their own vision and my students love going home with a finished piece that they designed."

Woven Gourd Centerpiece on an Iron Base by Deborah Mann. *Photography by Marianne Barnes.*

My husband, Jim, cuts and cleans my gourds. I know you are saying how lucky I am, and I am. Well, he got tired of throwing away the tops of the gourds so he came up with an idea. He flattened the bottom of the gourd top and glued it to a base. He makes the bases by cutting, sanding, and staining them. I love to wood-burn, so I decided to wood-burn designs on the gourd tops and added the color with oil pencil. There is a tutorial for wood-burned bowls and vases in Chapter 1. I decided the vases did not look finished and there was space left on the base, so I started adding embellishments to the base that accented what was wood-burned on the gourd. For example, I added a small ceramic frog to the vase titled *Frog*. On the base of the ocean gourd, I added real small shells that I found at Myrtle Beach, South Carolina. I even added a little sand from the beach.

TOP LEFT AND RIGHT:

Frog by Marianne Barnes. A miniature frog was used on the *Frog* base. *Photography by Kelly Hazel.*

BOTTOM LEFT AND RIGHT:

Shells by Marianne Barnes. Real shells and sand were used as embellishments. *Photography by Kelly Hazel.*

Gourd Jewelry

Women love jewelry, and gourd jewelry is so unique. The jewelry starts with a gourd base and the embellishments make them come alive.

Scrap Gourd Lady Pins by Chris Pace. *Photography by Kelly Hazel.*

Tutorials & Patterns

Scrap Gourd Lady Pins

BY CHRIS PACE

Chris Pace teaches a class called Scrap Gourd Lady Pins. Joe, Chris' husband, helps to put a special, two-part epoxy on the gourd pins when they are finished. Instructions for Chris' gourd pins follows.

THE PROJECT

Take pieces of a broken gourd, the flatter the better, and cut or sand to shape into irregular oval or round shapes. Any protrusions can be made into a hat or funky hairstyle! Perfection is not needed. For fun, paint a pin using the same hair and eye colors of a friend or relative, or maybe even yours.

Lady Gourd Pin by Terry Humphries. Photography by Kelly Hazel.

INSTRUCTIONS

- Sand the front of the gourd smooth and the back lightly. Also sand the sides of the gourd scrap. Wipe off all gourd dust. Make sure you wear a mask when sanding.

- Basecoat the front with a light color — white, tan, or flesh. You can paint the sides at this time or they do not have to be painted. *Note: You may want to paint the back of the scrap, too.*

- After the first coat of paint is completely dry, very lightly sand. If cool to the touch, it needs more drying time. I used a crumpled piece of plain brown paper bag for this sanding, but you can use fine 220 grit sandpaper, and sand lightly. Once again, wipe off any sanding dust, and wear a mask.

- Paint the final basecoat color. I suggest you use the flesh color of your choice. Paint the entire surface — front and, if applicable, sides. The back can be any color.

Eyes and Lips:

- Sketch the eyes or transfer an eye pattern, to make sure they will be the same size. Also transfer any other items that would be helpful to you, such as hat, hair, etc. Only sketch the outline. No details yet.
- Paint the entire eye white and let dry. Now you can paint the hair or hat area whatever background color you like. This will be the darker value of your hair or hat. Let dry.
- Use the handle end of a large paintbrush and "dot" the colored eye part on top of the white with a blue, green, or brown, if a natural eye color is desired. You may also paint this circled area instead if you wish.
- At the same time you are doing this and using the same, or slightly smaller, paintbrush handle, dot on the upper lips first and then the lower lips. I prefer my lower lips to be slightly bigger than the upper lips. These will be thick, so it will take longer to dry. Handle carefully so you don't smear the dots. Also, do not use a blow dryer on the dots as this will blow the paint.
- When the pin is completely dry, you can proceed. With an inky wash of black (paint mixed with a bit of water), use your liner brush to paint a thin line above and below the white of the eye, which will outline the whole eye. Use the same inky paint to add some eyelashes. You may also outline the round, colored part of the eye at this time.
- With the same inky black paint, draw a thin line from one side of the lips, curving up, then down a little, and then up out the other side. Look at the photograph. You can have your lady smile a lot or just slightly, or open her mouth just a bit and add upper teeth.
- With undiluted black paint, dab the end of a small paintbrush into the thick black and "dot" on the middle (iris) of the eye. Repeat on the other eye. Let it dry. With white paint, add a tiny dot to the upper corner of each eye — to the left or right of center (make sure you dot the SAME SIDE of each eye) — as a highlight. I use the tip of my liner brush for this, or the small end of my "stylus" tool.

Nose:

I prefer a brown, instead of black, for a little "suggestion" of nose and nostrils. Use a watered-down inky solution of brown, as you did for the eye outline, and wipe some of the paint off. Start at the top of the nose and pull down, with a slight curve, towards the direction you started on the side of the eye. Now, with undiluted brown, paint small nostrils (a slight "comma" stroke will do fine, or apply straight).

Eyebrows:

Use the brown, undiluted, to paint a hint of eyebrows above the eyes. *Note: You can also paint the eyebrows a similar color as the hair.*

Cheeks:

Stipple a light rose color on the cheek area. I like to load the stipple brush first and then dab onto a paper towel to get rid of most of the paint. You may use an old scruffy brush if you don't have a stipple brush. Let the pin dry completely.

Hair:

Gently drawing from a pattern, you can now use transfer paper to add detail. (Do not press hard or you will cause a crease, or dent, in the painted area.) Using the hair color and a lighter color, double load your brush and pull down from the top of the head to the bottom of the hair, making a slight "wiggle" motion for wavy hair. You will have some "streaks" in your hair. You can let this dry and add more if you wish.

Hat:

If you choose to paint a hat, you can paint this right over the hair if you want. If the hair is thick, you may want to sand the hat area lightly first and basecoat with the hat color. Let dry. Now paint the hat and add any cross-hatching (for a straw hat) or dots, or anything you want. When satisfied, let dry.

Adding Embellishments:

Add "bling," such as shiny, flat-back Swarovski™ crystals as a necklace and earrings, or other ways to make your pin "pop." Glue your bling on, let dry, and then seal the gourd pin.

LEFT AND RIGHT:

Chris and Joe Pace place the pins on the nails to cover with the two-part apoxie.

Joe uses the torch to dry the sealer.

(Photography by Kelly Hazel.)

Seal Gourd Pin:

There are two ways to seal your pin.

1. For ease and quickness, use a water-based sealer since we used Acrylic (water-based) paint. Brush (or spray) sealer on dry pin. Let dry and seal again. Let dry!

2. For a jewelry-type finish, use a two-part sealer, such as Envirotex Light®, which is available at most craft stores. Prior to sealing, you will need to come up with a way to hold the pin off the surface below. Be sure to cover the surface or use a disposable plate to catch any drips. One way to do this is by hammering three nails with large heads into a cheap block of wood, such as a 2" x 4" scrap, leaving the nails sticking up an inch or more. Place your gourd pin on top of the nails so it is stable when lightly touched.

DIRECTIONS

FOR THE TWO-PART SEALER:

- Have three clean, disposable containers, such as paper or plastic cups.
- Measure and mark inside two of these cups the same height (such as one inch).
- Pour "resin" to your mark in one cup and "hardener" in the second cup.
- Pour both the resin and hardener, at the same time, into the third cup and immediately begin mixing. Stir vigorously for two minutes, scraping the sides occasionally.
- Hold open cup away from your face. Do not breathe in the fumes. Small bubbles will form. This is normal.
- Now, pour the liquid onto your gourd scrap, the painted side, just enough to cover one scrap. *Note: The sealer will self-level, though you may need to scoot it around a bit with a popsicle stick.*
- Don't worry about bubbles! There will be more bubbles rising to the surface within a few minutes, and you will need to dissipate these in one of two ways: Breathing on your piece will cause the bubbles to disappear — you may need to do this for five minutes or more; keep checking (use good light!) for more bubbles rising. The second option is a blow torch. Hold the flame a few inches from your piece and "sweep" back and forth. It is not the heat or flame that takes away the bubbles, but the carbon dioxide, which is given off by a lit blow torch. That's why your breath can do as equally a good job; however, if you are doing more than a couple pins at a time it is easier on you to use a blow torch.
- During this same time, you should look for "drips" along the sides, using another popsicle stick to gently scrape these off as they form. I like the way the sealer seals the sides with this same shiny finish as long as the drips don't stick out below my pin.
- When all the bubbles and drips are gone, walk away and leave your pins where they are for two days or longer. This is a thick sealer that provides a coat equal to fifty coats of varnish. Because of the thickness, it takes a long time to cure.
- Glue on a pin back. Sign your name on the back and spray the back with a spray sealer. Wear with pride or give as a unique gift!

BY DEBBIE WILSON

MATERIALS

- Gourd shards cut into pin shapes
- #200, #400 wet dry sandpaper
- Water cup and water
- Wire #18 to 25 gauge for weaving and stringing the spokes
- Various types of yarns and strings for the weaving
- Wire cutters
- Trans Tint dyes or alcohol-based dyes
- Denatured alcohol
- Spray bottle
- Variety of beads and objects for embellishments

- Rotary tool with a three-fourth Inch drill bit
- Needle-nose pliers
- Scissors
- Paper towels
- Cotton swabs
- Backing material
- Pins, wire for slide

Woven gourd pin by Marianne Barnes.
Photography by Kelly Hazel.

INSTRUCTIONS

- Using your wet dry sandpaper, dip the #200 gauge in the water and sand shard on the sides and top, and then sand with the #400 gauge in the same way. It should feel really smooth and have luster. Buff with a paper towel.
- Apply Trans Tint dyes or inks. Using a cotton swab, add another color by dotting it on the first color. If still wet, one color will spread into the other one. You can do a gentle spray of denatured alcohol to help the colors bleed into each other.
- Allow to air dry or use a blow dryer. Spray with a fixative or use a quick-dry sealer.
- Trace backing material using the gourd shard as the pattern. Put the backing aside for now. Drill three to five holes where you want the weaving to start.
- Cut wire at least 1-1/2" longer than where you want the weaving to stop. Also look at the possibility of having the wire twist around the piece. Figure out your length based on how you want the weaving to go on the shard. Cut the number of wires you will need.

DIAGRAM 1:

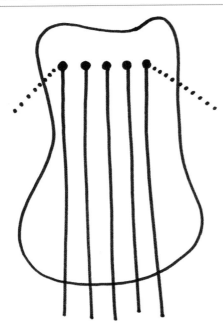

- Place spokes into the appropriate holes and bend them into the back. The needle-nose pliers will be helpful for this step. Only tuck in the top of the spokes and the bottom of the wire spokes will hang free as you weave.

DIAGRAM 2:

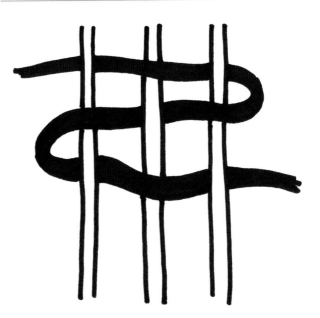

- Start weaving by using yarns in an under, over weave pattern.

DIAGRAMS 1 AND 2:

Scanned by Kelly Hazel.

DIAGRAM 3:

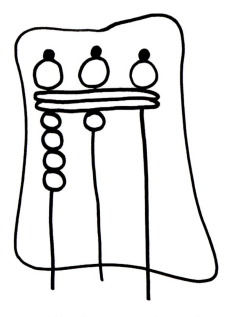

DIAGRAM 4:

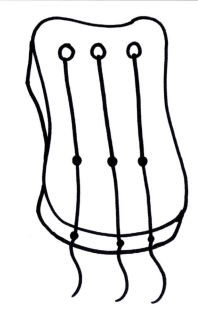

- You can add beads at any time by simply stringing them on the wire spokes and pushing them up. Keep a tight tension on the weaving.
- Continue weaving until you have reached the place you want to stop. Drill the appropriate number of holes and tuck the ends of the wire spokes into hole, bending back ends into gourd shard, or pull wire through holes and, if you have enough length, let these pieces of wire be your danglers.

- You may also drill holes into the bottom edge of the shard to make danglers of wire.

DIAGRAMS 3 AND 4:

Scanned by Kelly Hazel.

- Finish by stringing beads on danglers (if you want them) and making a rounded loop with the wire using the needle-nose pliers.
- Clip away any stray "hairs" from the yarn.

Beads on the danglers. *Photography by Kelly Hazel.*

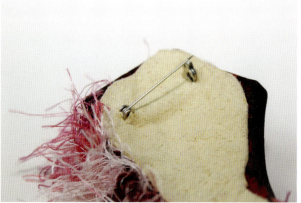

- Cut two holes for the pin in the backing material and slide to fit under the backing. Use leather and glue backing on the back of the shard to hide the wire.
- Allow to dry completely and wear.

Put a pin on the back. *Photography by Kelly Hazel.*

Holiday Gourds

LEFT AND RIGHT:

Caroling Mouse by Marianne Barnes. Photography by Kelly Hazel.

Miriam Joy made this cute mouse. Courtesy of Miriam Joy.

In this chapter, you will learn how to make ornaments, folk art angels, and recycled angels. I will also give you ideas for other ornaments following some of the same directions — just the embellishments will differ. This will be fun.

In one of our Patch meetings, Peggy Ash taught us how to make a caroling mouse ornament using Quickwood. Selma Carrow had sent Peggy a mouse for Christmas, as well as the instructions for making it. Since Peggy is our official "clay" member, she asked Selma for permission to teach the project with Peggy's adaptation.

Tutorials & Patterns

Mouse Christmas Ornament
by Selma Carrow

SUPPLIES

- Two jewelry gourds, one slightly smaller than the other, or you can use a jewelry gourd and a small egg gourd
- Quikwood — you could probably use air-dry clay as well, but I just prefer to use Quikwood
- Paint and brushes of your choice
- Other embellishments of your choice

DIRECTIONS

DIAGRAM 1:

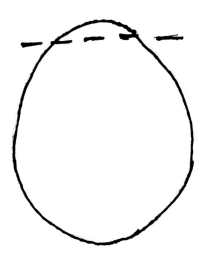

DIAGRAM 2:

- First, take the larger gourd (jewelry gourd or the egg gourd) and cut a small portion about the size of a dime off of the top (with the jewelry gourd you will be removing the long thin portion of the gourd). This will become the body of the mouse. The smaller gourd will now sit on top of this gourd.

- Next, work up a small portion of Quikwood and form a ball to secure the body and head together. Position

DIAGRAMS 1 AND 2:

Scanned by Kelly Hazel.

the head so that the long, narrow part of the gourd (which will be his nose) is slightly tipped upward; this will give the appearance that his head is tilted back. You can also use glue for this step, if you prefer.

- After the above step is dry, you can work on making the appendages for the mouse. You will need to make two arms, two feet, two ears, a tail, and a nose. All of these will be made out of Quikwood.

Arms:

Make two logs/ropes out of Quikwood, attach them to the upper portion of the body of the mouse, and bend forward toward the front. Using a toothpick, add creases for the bend of the arms; also make the ends of the arms into paws, so that they will be a little larger than the arm and a little round in shape. You will then need to make two marks, still using the toothpick, to form his toes/fingers. Front paws should be formed outward from the body as they will be holding a music book. You can crumple up a piece of plastic wrap to put between the arms in order to position them until they dry. Prior to them drying, you also will need to cut a slit in each of the paws to allow the music book to slip into the slit so he appears he is holding the book.

DIAGRAM 3:

Feet:

Using Quikwood, make two round balls about the size of dimes and attach to the bottom front of the gourd to form his feet. Using a toothpick, make two indentations in each foot in order to form the toes.

DIAGRAM 4:

Nose:

Using Quikwood, make a small round ball to form his nose and place at the end of the smaller gourd.

DIAGRAMS 3 AND 4:

Scanned by Kelly Hazel.

Ears:

Using Quikwood, make two round balls about the size of nickels. You will need to flatten these balls to form the ears. Take your thumb and place it in the middle of the ball to flatten, thereby forming an indentation in the ball. Be sure to leave room for the edge of the ear. You will then need to attach to the smaller gourd on each side to form his ears.

DIAGRAM 5:

Tail:

Using Quikwood, make a long, thin rope for the tail. Attach the larger end near the bottom of the body of the gourd. Here is where you can get creative. You can have your tail totally attached to the gourd or left out in the air or even let it rest on his arm. It is entirely up to you.

Now you will need to allow the mouse to completely dry prior to painting him. Once dry, you will paint him all gray, adding black for his nose. You will add the eyes, mouth, etc., per your preference.

DIAGRAM 6:

DIAGRAMS 5 AND 6:

Scanned by Kelly Hazel.

Tail can be shaped in different ways. *Photography by Kelly Hazel.*

Music Book:

Make a music book out of a tiny piece of cardstock, wrapping paper, or whatever you desire. Glue the book in the slits you made in his paws.

DIAGRAM 7:

Make a music book for the mouse to hold.
Photography by Kelly Hazel.

Scarf:

Cut out a small scarf and tie around the neck.

Continue to embellish, as desired, such as adding a Santa hat and fine wire or fishing line for whiskers, etc.

DIAGRAM 8:

DIAGRAMS 7 AND 8:

Scanned by Kelly Hazel.

Giraffe and Zebra Ornaments

BY LEE KLINE

Lee Kline makes giraffe and zebra ornaments. She is a marvelous painter, so I asked her to share her patterns. Using the same basic directions, other ornaments can also be created, such as a Christmas pickle, Rudolph the Red Nose Reindeer, and others.

Giraffe by Lee Kline.

Zebra by Lee Kline.

(Photography by Derral Durrence.)

MATERIALS

- Mini Chinese Bottle Gourd about 1-1/2" long. For the giraffe, you will want the gourd to have a little more waist. The zebra is shaped more like a little fat snowman, not so much of an indenture between the two sections.
- Banana Gourd 5" long
- Craft Glue (I use Weldbond)
- Eye hook
- Brushes: I prefer to use a 1/4- or 1/2-inch angle brush. Filberts, or round brushes, can be used.
- Toothpicks for the horns (Ossicones are giraffe horns).
- Quickwood or any air-dry clay: I prefer Quickwood because it does not chip easily.
- Dremel tool for drilling holes for the ears and the nubs or giraffe head
- Small scraps of leather or suede for ears, brown for giraffe and black for zebra
- Paint: *Giraffe* – Burnt sienna (spots, eye outline, horns, and muzzle), green (eye), black (pupil of eye and nostril), and white (white of eye and highlight); *Zebra* – White (basecoat the entire piece, white of eye, and highlight eye), black (eye outline, muzzle, and pupil of the eye), and blue, or whatever color you prefer (iris of the eye).
- Yarn: Eyelash yarn in brown for the giraffe and any other colors with texture. Use about five strands and twist them to form the mane. The zebra will have black eyelash yarn and about five other strands of different textured yarn (include a little white).

MAKING THE GIRAFFE

DIAGRAM 1:

- Begin by drilling a hole in the blossom end of a mini bottle gourd large enough to push the stem end of the banana gourd. Glue this and allow it to dry.
- I did not use a base coat on the giraffe. Using burnt sienna, begin to paint spots (remember, no two spots are alike.)

DIAGRAM 2:

- I begin at the blossom end and paint around the small spot on the bottom, working my way around and up.

Start painting spots at blossom end of giraffe. *Photography by Derral Durrence.*

DIAGRAMS 1 AND 2:

Scanned by Kelly Hazel.

DIAGRAM 3:

- Leave a small gap between your spots, allowing the gourd skin to show through.

- Paint spots all the way up the gourd; nearer the head, make them smaller, leaving a little larger space between them.

DIAGRAM 4:

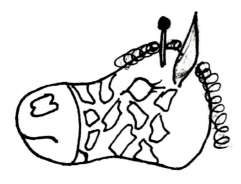

- Paint the muzzle with burnt sienna, nostrils with black that has been thinned with water similar to a wash, and draw a thin line for the mouth.

DIAGRAM 5:

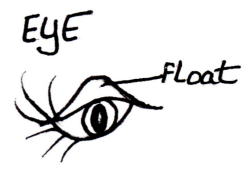

- Outline the eyes with burnt sienna, float over the top of the eyelid, paint some eyelashes, and fill the inside with white. When the white has dried, paint a circle of green, or whatever eye color you choose, paint the pupil black, and highlight with white.

DIAGRAMS 3, 4, 5, 6, AND 7:

Scanned by Kelly Hazel.

DIAGRAM 6:

- Drill holes for the horns on the head of the giraffe; glue the two toothpicks in place and allow to dry. Cut the toothpicks off, leaving about 1/2- to 3/4-inch. Make a small ball of Quickwood and place on the toothpicks. Allow this to dry and paint them burnt sienna. When dry, spray with clear acrylic spray.

DIAGRAM 7:

- Drill an "L"-shaped hole on each side of the top of the head for the ears on the outside of the nubs. Cut the ears out of leather; fold and glue into the hole. Take yarns and twist them together. Glue on the mane, starting between the horns on the head and going part way down the back. Drill a hole in the area of the head and neck near the mane; insert some glue and then your eyehook.

MAKING THE ZEBRA

DIAGRAM 1:

- Begin by drilling a hole in the mini bottle gourd on the round side of the gourd near the blossom end (see drawing). Have the hole large enough to fit the stem end of the banana gourd and glue; allow it to dry. Basecoat the entire piece white — it may take a couple of coats. Muzzle will be painted black; mix white and black to get gray for nostrils.

Zebra by Lee Cline. *Photography by Derral Durrence.*

DIAGRAM 1:

Scanned by Kelly Hazel.

DIAGRAM 2:

DIAGRAM 3:

- Outline the eyes with black, float over the top of the eyelid, paint some eyelashes, and fill the inside with white. When the white has dried, paint a circle of blue or whatever eye color you choose, paint the pupil black, and highlight with white.

- Paint wiggly lines on the face and around the body (going from the center of the back around to the stomach). Add shorter lines off of the lines you have already painted, all the way down the back of the gourd. When dry, coat with clear acrylic spray.

- Drill an "L"-shaped hole on each side of the top of the head for the ears. Cut the ears out of leather; fold and glue into the hole.

- Twist yarns together. Glue the mane, starting between the ears and going part way down the back. Drill a hole in the area of the head and neck near the mane; apply glue and insert eyehook into the hole.

Mane of zebra. *Photography by Derral Durrence.*

DIAGRAMS 2 AND 3:

Scanned by Kelly Hazel.

Reindeer

by Laraine Short

This is a pattern very similar to Lee's giraffe and zebra. When I was visiting Laraine in Florida, she taught me how to make a reindeer ornament. It differs from Lee's pattern only by the embellishments used and color of the ornament.

Reindeer by Marianne Barnes. Original pattern came from Laraine Short. *Photography by Kelly Hazel.*

MATERIALS

- Banana gourd and jewelry gourd (mini Chinese bottle gourd or Tennessee spinner)
- Quickset glue
- Drill
- Paint: Medium to dark brown for body; red or black for nose; black, white, and your choice of eye color for eyes
- Small scraps of brown leather, fur, or yarn for tail
- Small scraps of material for scarf
- Mini Christmas lights (look in Christmas section or dollhouse section at a craft store)
- Eyehook and ribbon or cording for hanger

INSTRUCTIONS

DIAGRAM 1:

DIAGRAM 2:

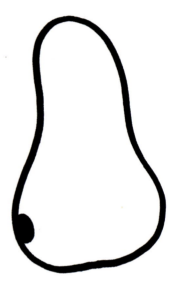

- Choose a banana gourd and a jewelry gourd that go together well.

- Drill a hole in the bottom of the head when you hold the gourd sideways (see dot on the diagram). Place the small end of the banana gourd into the head hole and make sure they fit. Glue together.

- Basecoat the body a medium to dark brown. Let dry.
- Paint on the eyes. I paint a white eye shape by putting a curve line at top and bottom of the eye. Fill in white color. Let dry.
- Choose color of eye (blue, brown, black, or green) and paint in small circle in middle of eye. It should touch the top and bottom of the curved lines. Outline the top and bottom of eye with black paint. Add eyelashes and an eyebrow. Place a tiny dot in each eye at the top left or right (same direction in both eyes).
- Paint nose red or brown.
- Use black to make a mouth under the nose.
- Optional: I like to paint a small heart on the body.
- Drill a small hole and screw in an eyehook. Tie ribbon on eyehook as hanger. Spray with sealer.

DIAGRAMS 1 AND 2:

Scanned by Kelly Hazel.

- Drill two small holes in top of head near the place where the stem was. Glue black wire into the holes. I also used another shorter piece of wire to twist on long piece at the top for the antler; to do this, twist the small wire around the long wire and put a drop of glue to hold. Now, take the mini Christmas lights and wrap from one antler to the other. I sometimes add drops of glue to hold them to the wire. Take a small piece of brown leather and cut out two ears (see Lee's pattern for shape). Drill two holes in the head next to the antlers and glue in the ears. If you wish, tie a small piece of cloth around the neck for a scarf.

TOP LEFT AND RIGHT:

Basecoat the reindeer a medium to dark brown.

Paint eyes and nose.

(Photography by Kelly Hazel.)

Christmas Pickle Ornament

by Laraine Short

Pickle by Marianne Barnes. Original pattern from Laraine Short. *Photography by Kelly Hazel.*

MATERIALS

- Banana Gourd
- Hot melt glue and glue stick
- Green paint (I like a darker green), black, red, and white
- Paint brushes – medium flat and liner
- Cord or ribbon for hanging
- Drill

INSTRUCTIONS

DIAGRAM 1:

- Paint the entire gourd green except for the tip. Paint the tip white and red to look like a Santa hat (or you can just paint it all green with no hat).
- Let dry. While you are waiting for it to dry, heat the hot melt glue gun. When the gourd is dry and hot melt gun is hot, drop dots of glue along the body, resembling the protrusions of a pickle.
- Paint the eyes by making a black teardrop. When dry, paint a curved white shape at the bottom of the eyes. Put a small dot in the top of the eyes.

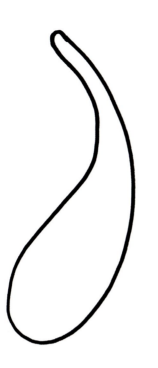

Scanned by Kelly Hazel.

Close-up of face of pickle. *Photography by Kelly Hazel.*

Laraine provided a tag to attach to the Christmas Pickle that reads on one side:

> "Legend of the Christmas Pickle"
> In Old World Germany it was traditional to hang the Christmas Pickle last, hidden among the branches. The first child on Christmas Day to find the Christmas Pickle receives a special blessing for the year and an extra gift.

On the opposite side type the following:

> Today Grandma doesn't like to leave any child out. So on Christmas Day EACH child that finds the Christmas Pickle and whispers in Grandma's ear where it is, receives a special blessing and a special Candy Cane.

GALLERY

Other Holiday Gourds

Here are some other ideas for making holiday ornaments or trinkets with banana gourds.

The first holiday gourd I made was a Santa. I took a class with Sammy Crawford at the first Cherokee Gourd Gathering. The entire gourd is white, except the face area. Gray was added to make the beard and mustache. The face was painted with flesh and the eyes, nose, and mouth were added. The entire gourd was sealed with a spray sealer. A small white feathery piece was added as an embellishment and a small red cloth rose and red bell were added. I still hang it on my tree every Christmas.

Elegant Santa by Marianne Barnes.
Photography by Kelly Hazel.

I made the Grinch ornament as a request from a friend. I painted it green except for the hat and coat, which was painted red and white. I used black paint for the features and white for the eyes. Laraine Short made the snowmen. Laraine is a decorative painter and is very skilled in painting. She adds embellishments like scarves and pompoms for the top of the hats. Peggy Hoffmaster painted the elf. She is also a decorative painter. Each year, members of Peggy's painting group exchange hand-painted Christmas ornaments. Peggy used a wood heart and painted it black for the feet and attached the banana gourd to it — a very clever embellishment.

ABOVE: LEFT TO RIGHT

The Grinch by Marianne Barnes.

Snowman with Scarf by Laraine Short.

Snowman by Laraine Short.

(Photography by Kelly Hazel.)

Elf by Peggy Hoffmaster. Photography by Kelly Hazel.

I created this pumpkin man with a small banana gourd. I used an X-Acto knife and cut out the eyes, nose, mouth, and one tooth. I used dyes to paint the body, except for the tooth, which was painted with white after the dye dried. *Note: The inside of the gourd was left unclean so you can see the fibers that need to be removed.*

Pumpkin Man by Marianne Barnes.
Photography by Kelly Hazel.

Laraine Short's candy corn decoration utilizes an egg gourd. A wood heart, painted yellow, serves as a stand.

Candy Corn by Laraine Short.
Photography by Kelly Hazel.

Betty Bloomfield used a larger banana gourd to create this witch for Halloween. She used Quickwood for the features of the face and the arms and hands. She attached the gourd to a base of Quickwood. The broom is a stick with raffia and the hair is dyed felting. The hats can be purchased at a craft store.

Witch by Betty Bloomfield.
Photography by Kelly Hazel.

Snowballs are very easy ornaments to make. Select a round gourd or a squash-shaped gourd, paint it white, and add some facial features and pink cheeks. Spray with a sealer and add an eyehook and a cord for hanging. Sometimes I hot-glue a Christmas decoration at the top of the head or use spray glue and sprinkle glitter or loose snow (purchased from a craft store). I also wood-burned some egg gourds as Santas and added color with an oil pencil.

LEFT: TOP TO BOTTOM

Snowball by the author. Original design by Peggy Ash.

Wood-burned Santa balls by Marianne Barnes.

RIGHT: TOP TO BOTTOM

Christmas sprig added to a snowball head.

Squash-shaped gourd snowball.

(Photography by Kelly Hazel.)

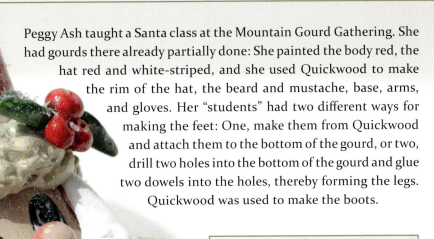

Peggy Ash taught a Santa class at the Mountain Gourd Gathering. She had gourds there already partially done: She painted the body red, the hat red and white-striped, and she used Quickwood to make the rim of the hat, the beard and mustache, base, arms, and gloves. Her "students" had two different ways for making the feet: One, make them from Quickwood and attach them to the bottom of the gourd, or two, drill two holes into the bottom of the gourd and glue two dowels into the holes, thereby forming the legs. Quickwood was used to make the boots.

CLOCKWISE:

Santa with a clay beard by Peggy Ash. Peggy uses dowels for Santa's legs and Quickwood for his boots. *Photography by Kelly Hazel.*

I love to wood-burn, so many of my Christmas gourds have wood-burned designs. I like to make oil lamps and I wood-burn a Christmas or winter scene on the front of the gourd. Using cannonball or small canteen gourds, drill a hole the size of a glass oil lamp insert. Clean out the inside of the gourd. This is when I burn a scene: I used oil pencils to add color and sprayed the gourd with a fixative and then spray sealer. Add textured snow. Unless the gourd is placed on a stand for stability, you can add sand to give weight and balance to the gourd. Place the glass insert in the hole. The addition of raffia around the glass insert makes it look a little more festive.

LEFT AND TOP RIGHT:

The Little Church in the Vale by Marianne Barnes. The design on the cannonball gourd was wood-burned and colored in with an oil pencil. *Photography by Kelly Hazel.*

BOTTOM RIGHT:

Oil lamp with hole in the top for glass insert. *Photography by Kelly Hazel.*

International award-winning gourd artist Lynette Dawson specializes in gourd embroidery. Lynette and her daughter were responsible for the compilation and construction of the Gourd Patch Quilt found at this link: www.americangourdsociety.org/quilt. Lynette and I participated in a gourd exchange and I received this beautiful Valentine bowl that she created. The red hearts are stitched on the gourd and the white hearts are painted. The inside of the bowl is red. I was very excited to receive this gourd and keep it in my special gourd collection.

TOP TO BOTTOM:

Hearts by Lynette Dawson. *Courtesy of Lynette Dawson.*

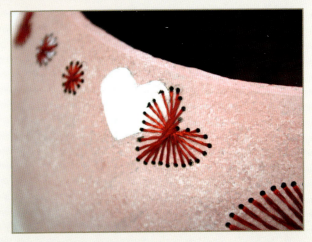

Folk Art, Recycled, & Old World Angels

Many Christmas ornaments today are Folk Art or Old World styles. They can be simple or very elaborate. Angels are also a subject highly used at this time of the year. Many of the ornaments at Christmastime are hand-made and treasured by family and friends.

Folk Art Angel by Debbie Wilson. *Photography by* Kelly Hazel.

Tutorials & Patterns

Folk Art Angel
by Debbie Wilson

Debbie Wilson is an artist who specializes in folk art. She started making angels using gourds and recycled materials, and sells them at galleries and shows.

Folk Art Angels by Debbie Wilson. Debbie dyes, carves, and adds embellishments to create each different angel. *Photography by Kelly Hazel.*

MATERIALS

- Bottle gourd that will balance and sit flat
- Dremel or power carver
- Small dental bits
- Round reed for wings (three to a side)
- Twine or string for weave
- Sisal, pine needles, jute, seagrass, or whatever you want to use for hair
- Pencil
- Dye and Acrylic spray sealer

INSTRUCTIONS

Dye the entire gourd one color and let dry. Spray with a sealer.

DIAGRAM 1:

- With your pencil, draw an oval for the location of the face in front of the gourd.

DIAGRAM 2:

- Draw in facial features and make them large to fill the space. Be sure to leave room for the chin below the lips. Draw in the lines for the bottom of the cheekbone and lines under the nose.

DIAGRAMS 1 AND 2:

Scanned by Kelly Hazel.

DIAGRAM 3:

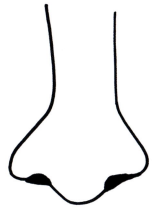

- Drill or carve two tiny nostrils under the end of the nose.

DIAGRAM 4:

CARVING:

- Carve the outline of the oval of the face with a straight dental bit.
- Outline all facial figures, including the mark under the cheekbones. Don't carve too deep.
- Start carving away under the cheeks, first sloping upward.
- Cut deeper down the sides of the nose and then carve toward the cheek. Refer to the diagram.
- Cut away above the eyebrow and, using strokes, cut away skin to top of circle.
- Cut away all skin of the gourd, leaving eyebrows and eyes with the dyed gourd showing. Lightly take off dye around the mouth. Lightly take away where the eyeball goes in.
- Under the mouth, take the chin skin off and, sloping around and under, round it off. Round off the sides of the nose and cheeks. Refer to the diagram.

DIAGRAMS 3 AND 4:

Scanned by Kelly Hazel.

Wings:

Diagram 5:

- Drill three holes on back near the shoulder. This is where the reed will be inserted for the wings.

Diagram 6:

- After drilling, glue the reed in the holes.

Weaving:

Diagram 7:

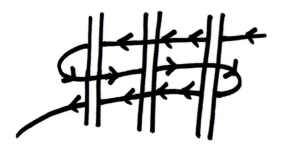

- Weave every other spoke under, over, turn around last spoke, over, under, etc. Refer to the diagram. Weave until you get to within 1/4" to the top of the three pieces of reed.

Weave the wings of the angel. *Photography by Kelly Hazel.*

DIAGRAMS 5, 6, AND 7:

Scanned by Kelly Hazel.

DIAGRAM 8:

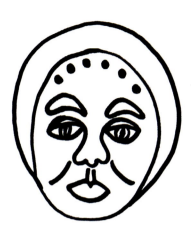

- For the hair, drill holes or use an awl to make four to seven holes. An uneven number seems to work better. Insert and glue sisal, pine needles, jute, seagrass, or whatever you want to use for hair. Trim, if needed.

- To make a halo, use reed or sisal and make a circle. Wind material around itself on each side to keep it in place. Glue to the back of the head.

DIAGRAM 8:

Scanned by Kelly Hazel.

TOP RIGHT AND BOTTOM:

Debbie used sisal for the hair.

Make a halo for the back of the head.

(Photography by Kelly Hazel.)

Recycled Angels

Choose recycled materials to make these angels. Some recycled materials used were assorted aluminum soda cans (cut out) and assorted bottle caps (flattened). For the hands, kudzu, palm stems, metal brackets, nails, and tabs from soda pop cans were used. Legs were made from small pieces of honeysuckle vine. Gourd shards were used for the bodies, which were then wood-burned with an addition of inks or acrylic paints. Rings and eye screws were used to attach legs to the body.

The gourd shards were cut to make a smaller head and larger body with a neck. The cans were cut to make wings, hearts, birds, flowers, and halos. The honeysuckle legs were painted and the eye screws and rings were used to attach them to the body so they will move. Holes were drilled in the top of the head and the hair was glued in. Inks and acrylic paint were used for facial features.

TOP TO BOTTOM:

Recycled Angels by Debbie Wilson.

On this angel, Debbie used a Dr. Pepper can for the wings.

(Photography by Kelly Hazel.)

TOP: LEFT TO RIGHT:

Pop top cap used for a head.

For this angel, palm stems were used for the hair.

A small piece of gourd is cut in a circle and used for the face of the angel. The features are drawn on the gourd.

(Photography by Kelly Hazel.)

This angel has nails for hair. *Photography by Kelly Hazel.*

TOP

Triangle-shaped gourd body and kudzu hair. *Photography by Kelly Hazel.*

BOTTOM LEFT AND RIGHT:

The honeysuckle legs are painted and attached with rings.

Close-up of how the legs are attached.

(Photography by Kelly Hazel.)

Old World Angels

Debbie Wilson also made these Old World Angels with gourd shards shaped like angels. She added wings with wire by drilling holes in the top sides of the gourd shards and gluing the wire bent wings in the holes. The legs and halos were also bent and glued into the holes. The angels were painted with ink and acrylic paints.

TOP

Old World Angels by Debbie Wilson.
Photography by Kelly Hazel.

LEFT TO RIGHT:

Debbie used heavy gauge wire for the wings of the angels.

Detail of drawing visible through the white wash.

(Photography by Kelly Hazel.)

Knots

This chapter is about knots. Maybe you have never thought about using knots on a gourd as an embellishment. Donna Crispin loves to make Japanese knots, and has authored a book on them. All of the knots featured here can be made on gourds by drilling holes at the proper locations.

> **TOP TO BOTTOM:**
>
> Spiral cross knot or Juji-uzamaki-musub by Donna Crispin.
>
> Double interlocking V knot with circle by Donna Crispin.
>
> Double interlocking V knot by Donna Crispin.
>
> *(Courtesy of Donna Crispin.)*

Tutorials & Patterns

Cross Knot and Turtle Shell Knot

BY DONNA CRISPIN

Donna adds the knot to a gourd.

We will start off with the Cross Knot, Juji-musubi, and then add on the Turtle Shell Knot, Kame-no-ko-musubi. (All images courtesy of Donna Crispin.)

MATERIALS

- Prepared gourd
- Cane (I used two different types and sizes, but this isn't necessary.)
- Drill
- Scissors
- Pencil
- Measuring tape
- Awl
- Large eyed needle
- Old towel

Part 1–Cross Knot:

Cut two pieces of cane at 17". Soak the cane in water for about five minutes. Put one piece of cane in a towel.

Step 1:

Mark gourd with a pencil, and then drill 4 holes in the gourd about 1" apart.

Step 2:

Cut points in both ends of one of the pieces of cane. Start inside the gourd, bringing the long end out of the lower left corner hole, shiny side up. Leave about a 1" tail inside the gourd. Take the long end to the upper right corner hole and insert. Pull tightly, so the cane lays flat against the gourd. On the inside, bring the cane over to the upper left corner hole and pull it out.

Step 3:

Insert the cane in the lower right corner hole, forming an "X."

Step 4:

On the inside, bring the cane to the lower left corner hole and out again. Try to cover the short end of the cane inside, so that it's not hanging loosely.

STEP 5:

Insert the cane into the upper right corner hole, then across (inside) to the upper left corner hole, and out. From the upper left corner, head towards the lower right corner, going over, then under the cross pieces of the X. You may need an awl here. Insert the end into the lower right corner hole. Tuck and cut the end.

Part 2–Turtle Shell Knot

STEP 6:

Cut points on both ends of the second piece of cane. Start by tucking the short end under the X, shiny side up. Weave counter-clockwise, in an over-under pattern, using all eight pieces of the cross. You might want to use your awl here to loosen up the cross a bit. Be careful not to scratch your gourd. I was able to thread the second piece of cane onto a large eyed needle, which helped quite a bit.

STEP 7:

Continue weaving around in the same manner, as many times as you like.

STEP 8:

When you are done, tuck the long end under the knot and cut it off.

GALLERY OF COMPLETED PROJECTS

TOP LEFT AND RIGHT:

Gourd was made by Maggie LeDuc.

Butterflies by Maggie LeDuc.

(Courtesy of Maggie LeDuc.)

BOTTOM LEFT AND RIGHT:

Waves by Dr. Linda Lake. 9" x 8". She used a tooled leather rim and feathers for embellishments. *Courtesy of Dr. Linda Lake.*

Swimming in the Pond by Marianne Barnes. *Photography by Kelly Hazel.*

TOP LEFT AND RIGHT:

Blue Jay by Debbie Wilson. *Photography by Kelly Hazel.*

Maggie LeDuc used a shell as an embellishment. *Photography by Maggie LeDuc.*

BOTTOM LEFT AND RIGHT:

Betsey Sloan's jewelry with stone and silver wire. *Photography by Kelly Hazel.*

Tenerife by Ruth Clingingbeard. I wanted to use her beautiful gourd as a memorial to her. *Photography by Kelly Hazel.*

Biographies of Contributing Artists

Wayne Anderson

Wayne Anderson started working with gourds in 2000 after he met his wife, Patricia. He saw a few gourds his wife had painted and was impressed. He started by painting a few gourds and then decided to expand his art to weaving copper and sewing designs around the rim, to create very unique bowls. The first gourds he created were gifts for his wife and other family members. Wayne is self-employed and does drywall and contract work. His hobbies are playing guitar, writing songs, wire-wrapping gemstones, collecting rocks and gemstones, and most of all spending time with his grandchildren.

Peggy Ash

I'm a native Michigander and found my way to gourds by chance/accident. I have loved and tried many art forms since an early age, but the one that stuck was my love of all things clay. I love polymer, Quickwood, Apoxie Sculpt, and paper clay. I also make my own clays. They all can be incorporated into working with gourds. My sister had given me some dried ornamental gourds that she had forgotten about in her garage from Thanksgiving (this was in the late '90s). Since I had covered light-bulbs with clay, she was sure I could do something with those gourds. I did. I made Santa's, which are still one of my favorites to do.

Finding gourds in Michigan was no easy task. The ones I did find either rotted (picked too early) or were very thin-shelled. Plus no one seemed to speak gourd! I turned to Ebay® often and learned as much as I could from the Internet (online Gourd Patch). I had just met a few folks from various parts of Michigan and Indiana that did gourd work or grew gourds when low and behold my husband took a job in South Carolina. Because of the move, I was finally able to go to the Cherokee Gourd Gathering, took my first class, and met like-minded folks who I am privileged to call friends still today. I also met Marianne Barnes, who was trying to get a gourd patch together near where I lived. I barged my way

in and began exploring many new facets to the never-ending art medium known as a "gourd." I have learned to carve (thanks, in no small part, to Bonnie Gibson), burn (long story), and I even attempted to weave a little (weaving challenged). I have been so lucky to have taught and taken classes in Florida, Georgia, South Carolina, and North Carolina.

I have met some of the most fantastic, artistic, creative, sharing folks through gourds and made some marvelous lifelong friends — and all because of a moldy vegetable.

Gail Bishop

I am a native Californian. I love nature, animals, outdoors, and art! I am blessed with the support of my family, my husband of thirty-seven years, Barry, and blessed with my loving daughter, Michelle. After being diagnosed with Rheumatoid Arthritis, I pushed myself further into my artwork for physical and mental relief. My art led me on a wonderful new path, to a fulfilling journey in life.

Betty Bloomfield

Betty has always been a crafter in one way or another, whether painting, knitting, sewing, or making jewelry. She has been puttering with gourds for about twelve years, after discovering gourd art at the North Carolina Folk Art Center. She took a gourd basket class.

Says Betty: "What an adventure it has been, best of all meeting and making new friends in the gourd world. What we can create with a gourd is limitless and I love every aspect of it. Today I'm still on a continuing gourd education quest."

Betty has taught gourd classes at various festivals and gatherings in South Carolina, Georgia, Florida, Tennessee, and Indiana. She is married, lives on a lake with her husband and cat (Maddie Bright), and has four children and eight grandchildren. She is retired from the Greenville County School District and is a member of the Palmetto Gourd Patch, South Carolina Gourd Society, and American Gourd Society.

Karen Hundt Brown

I was born in Niles, Michigan, and moved to the farm where I was raised while my mom was expecting my sister. I didn't know I had ADD as a kid…I just knew I was a very active child, so my parents stuck me in 4-H and told me to take classes. I took all kinds of classes, which kept me busy and out of trouble. After high school (where I earned a Golden Key award in art), I attended Southwestern Michigan College for a year, majoring in art and English. I transferred to Kendall School of Art and Design a year later, where I studied illustration for two years before dropping out. I knew I couldn't make it drawing all the time when there were so many other types of art out there to play with.

Years later, I met and married my husband and, when we moved into our home, I started a garden the first spring.

With the first seed order, I got a free packet of gourd seeds. Having never seen or grown a gourd before, I had to try them. I got fifty gourds that first year and didn't know what to do with them. I went to the local library and took out *The Complete Gourd* by Widess and Summit, where I found I had six months to a year for the gourd to dry before I could start making stuff out of them. I read everything our library system had on gourds and then went online to find out even more — that's where I found the American Gourd Society and all its chapters. I found out that Ohio's show was the same weekend as my birthday and I was not going to miss that, so I called for a show book and started planning my fist competition pieces in years. I entered twenty-two pieces and brought home eleven ribbons and the rest is history. I was hooked!

We still live in Alaska, Michigan, with our kitty kids and I still garden and grow gourds (at least one variety) most years. I try to find new and interesting projects to make for classes to teach, and I am always on the lookout for new and interesting items and techniques to try on my gourds. I still take classes — mostly carving classes right now — to learn new things to try on my gourds and to become a better carver.

I sand all my gourds inside and out to get them as smooth as possible before any stain/dye goes on so that when I apply the finish it will not need to be sanded off and reapplied several times in order to get the inside of the gourd smooth. I know all this sanding seems like a lot of extra work, but it is the difference between first and second place in competition and more money as a sellable piece of artwork.

Selma Carrow

Selma has been participating in arts and crafts since she was very young. Her mother always encouraged her to be creative. She has mastered a variety of arts and crafts in her past and still works at incorporating other media in her gourd work. She has been working on gourds since 1996 and is a member of the American Gourd Society and the Florida Gourd Society.

Selma was the show chair for the Florida Gourd Show for five years. She also, five years ago, created, organized, and conducted a Florida Fall Gourd Retreat event, which she continues to host with the assistance of many other artists and the support of the Florida Gourd Society.

Selma has a Bachelors Degree in Criminal Justice and loves the outlet of working on her crafts after working all day in her profession. She encourages others to be creative and loves the

camaraderie with other gourd artists and learning new and different techniques. She is influenced by a variety of textures and loves to work with natural items the most.

Ruth Clinkingbeard

Ruth was a member of the Palmetto Gourd Patch. She was involved in many arts and crafts all her life. Ruth passed away in 2012 and has been greatly missed. She was so much fun and was always smiling and encouraging the members to be creative! We celebrate her life and honor her in this book.

Donna Crispin

Donna has been creating baskets and teaching workshops since 1986. As a former park ranger, she has lived in some of the most beautiful places in the western United States. Although she is now living in an urban area, her pieces often reveal

the spiritual and physical connection she has developed from her time spent in nature.

Her interests in Japanese and Native American cultures have also been a large influence in her baskets and other woven pieces. She is an advocate of continuing education and has taken many basketry workshops, along with ceramics, jewelry, and weaving. This background has allowed her to develop a unique, personal style, which she enjoys sharing with others.

Brenda L. Dewald

Brenda L. Dewald is a fiber artist with a special interest in working with gourds and pine needles. Brenda's inspiration for her earthy and nature-based artwork comes from everyday experiences on her Oklahoma ranch.

Brenda's interest in art began in junior high school when her mother enrolled her in a weekly oil painting class. As a sophomore in high school, Brenda was awarded the Grand Champion art ribbon at the Oklahoma State Fair.

Since that time, Brenda's interest has shifted to fiber art. Today, she can be found in her home studio perfecting the handcraft skill of ink dyeing, sculpting, and hand-stitching unique, beautiful gourd and pine needle art. Brenda completes her artwork by signing, numbering, and archiving each piece before offering it to collectors and galleries.

She is inspired by, and has studied under, numerous oil painting artists, fiber artists, and gourd artists. Her most memorable study experiences are with oil paint artists Jim Wilcox of Jackson, Wyoming, and Dennis Parker of Oklahoma City, Oklahoma; fabric artists Sharon Yoder of Kingfisher, Oklahoma, and Randi Parrish of Hennessey, Oklahoma; and gourd artists John Hernandez of Lawton, Oklahoma, and Don Weeke of Julian, California.

Brenda shows her artwork at exhibitions, festivals, museums, and galleries. Her 2012 events and awards include the Western Design Conference & Show in Jackson, Wyoming; Award of Excellence at the Arts Festival Oklahoma in Oklahoma City, Oklahoma; Best of Show at Firehouse Art Center Midsummer Nights' Fair in Norman, Oklahoma; Best of Show at Paso Arts Festival in Oklahoma City, Oklahoma; Honorable Mention 3D Art at Downtown Edmond Arts Festival, Edmond, Oklahoma; Second Place in the Master's Division at the California Gourd Society Competition, Fallbrook, California; Kerr Arts & Cultural Center Southwest Gourd Fine Art Show in Kerrville, Texas; Arts and Preservation in the Osage in Pawhuska, Oklahoma; Hillsboro Arts & Crafts Fair in Hillsboro, Kansas; NRHA Derby and the NRHA Futurity in Oklahoma City, Oklahoma; Frontier Country Museum in Crescent, Oklahoma; The Muse, Fred Jones Jr. Museum of Art Gift Gallery in Norman, Oklahoma.

In 2011, Brenda was awarded the Oklahoma Visual Arts Association Professional Basics Grant and Education Grant. Her artwork was featured on the cover of the 2011-2012 *Welburn Gourd Farm Catalog* and has appeared in numerous blog and Internet sites and newsprint publications.

Brenda is affiliated with numerous professional organizations. She holds a BA degree in Agriculture from Oklahoma State University. Her teaching schedule and artwork are available through her website, bdewaldfinearts.com.

Kristy Dial

I fell in love with gourds almost twenty years ago because of the artistic possibilities; I saw the gourd as a gift from nature and a wonderfully unique canvas. Being born and raised in Tucson, Arizona, my appreciation of Native American art started at an early age. My family and I have explored countless rock art sites, attended Pow Wows, and visited Pueblos of the Southwest to enhance my art. I strive to honor the gourd and to celebrate the American Indian culture in each piece.

My work has evolved over the years to incorporate several techniques. Besides introducing torching as a technique used on gourds, I am also excited about integrating embossed copper and patinas into my work. I draw inspiration from fellow artists and from the art of the American Indians. Most of my gourds are torched, pyroengraved, carved, and enriched with dyes and acrylics.

In addition to exhibiting in art shows, I teach a variety of classes in California, Nevada, Arizona, Florida, Idaho, and Texas. My work is also on display in galleries in Arizona, California, Utah, and Wyoming.

Lynette Dawson

Lynette Dawson of Michigan has been creating gourd art since 1998. In 2002, she started embroidering on the gourd, which has won her many ribbons and awards at gourd shows across the United States. Her embroidery work has also been featured in newspapers and magazines.

Iris Durand

I went to a local craft show here in Brevard, North Carolina, about fifteen years ago, where I saw, and then bought, my very first gourd, which had been painted by Karen Dittman. The fact that it was a natural object with the seeds still rattling around inside intrigued me. I signed up right away when our local Arts Council offered a two-day workshop taught by Karen. It was a "crash" course that included cleaning, cutting, drilling, and painting. I went home with four unfinished gourds — and the inspiration and confidence to keep on "gourding."

I eventually heard about, and then joined, the Asheville Gourd Patch (who would ever have imagined such a club?) and then, luckily, I happened on a weaving class taught by Marianne Barnes and found my way to her Palmetto Gourd Patch in Greenville, South Carolina. I had thought I had already seen and heard of all that can be done with gourds, but this group has opened up a whole new world of ideas, fun, and other gourd events.

Charlotte Durrence

I painted my first gourd in 1993 and have been consumed by the desire to do many more. I still have that first gourd. It reminds me of all that I have learned over the years. I am a charter member of the Georgia Gourd Society and have held many offices in the organization. I served as first Vice-President of the American Gourd Society for one term.

Teaching gourd art classes has taken me all over the country and I have met so many wonderful people with the same interest. My husband, Derral, has been a great supporter in all the things that I do. I love doing pine needle weaving and natural gourds.

Stu Fabe

Stu Fabe has been a full-time artist since 2004 specializing in fine art gourds, which he and his partner, Marla Helton, have grown on their 36-acre farm near Greencastle, Indiana. Prior to devoting himself to his art career, Stu was a fundraising executive for twenty-five years for major charities, including the Cincinnati Children's Hospital, the Cincinnati Zoo, and Health Alliance of Cincinnati.

Stu's technique involves coil weaving with Danish cord and waxed linen thread. After cleaning and richly coloring the gourds with dyes and other pigments, he cuts abstract openings and then creates a natural, sculptural effect by tightly weaving the Danish cord. His pieces are often mounted onto beautiful hardwood bases as pieces of sculpture. Other works are wall-mounted pieces of woven sculpture, while still others are gourds woven in-the-round.

In addition to his fine gourds, Stu has published five books, including the very popular *Wild Women of Gourdonia*, a collection of whimsical stories about "Wild Women" as fanciful beings crafted from pieces of hard-shell gourds. Additionally, Stu has been a serious photographer for nearly forty years. He has had five solo exhibitions of his images and has published two photography books.

Stu exhibits his gourd art in galleries and art shows, mainly throughout the Midwest. His artwork is owned by numerous corporate and private collectors and has been featured in several books on gourd art. Stu and Marla have won numerous awards in art shows, and he was named as a finalist in the category of Decorative Fiber for the 2007 Niche Awards. His gourd art was also featured on the cover of the November 2008 issue of *Sunshine Artist*.

Ruth Gedroic

Ruth Gedroic has primarily worked and exhibited in photography and the quilting arts. In exploring the creative process, Ruth has developed an interest in and experimented with pine needle basketry and gourd art. She chooses to gather and use natural materials found in the environment to emphasize and complement her work. For her, the acquisition of technical skills in three-dimensional work serves as a welcome challenge from those familiar in two-dimensional media.

Bonnie Gibson

Bonnie is a highly sought-after and well-respected instructor who has taught gourd carving and crafting classes for many years. Bonnie travels extensively, teaching workshops from coast to coast. Her website, ArizonaGourds.com, is a major source of gourd crafting supplies, tools, tutorials, and information. Her book *Gourds: Southwestern Techniques and Projects*, published in 2006, is now available in a paperback edition with a new title: *Gourds with Southwestern Motifs*. Bonnie has earned many

awards in different media, including multiple "Best of Show" awards. Certain gourd techniques and design elements, such as carved sand ripples, filigree, and basketry effects, have become her signature patterns.

Says Bonnie: "Gourds are a versatile canvas for expressing my love of nature and native cultures. My work reflects the world that surrounds me; living in the southwest for over thirty years has provided me with an endless source of inspiration. A lifelong interest in many diverse forms of artistic media, including woodcarving, scale miniatures, paints, glass, and clay, have influenced my work with gourds and provided me with valuable experiences and technical abilities. One of my primary goals is to help lift gourds out of the realm of 'crafts' and into greater acceptance as fine art. To that end, I enjoy manipulating gourds in new ways, inviting the viewer to interpret them as something more while retaining their natural essence.

"I enjoy teaching classes and sharing what I have learned with others. Educating others about gourd art led me to writing *Gourds: Southwest Gourd Techniques & Projects from Simple to Sophisticated*, recently released by Sterling Publishing. My goal as a teacher and author is to provide other gourd artists with technical skills while inspiring them to stretch their boundaries and view gourds from a new perspective."

COOKIE HANSON

Cookie Hanson is a well-known California fiber artist who has been exploring basketry techniques since the 1970s. Primarily engaged in basket making, Cookie also explores the intersection of gourds and fiber, as well as free-form sculpture, using both traditional and gathered natural materials. She is an active member of Bay Area Basket Makers, Los Angeles Basketry Guild, Misty Washington Basket and Gourd Guild (San Diego), and California Gourd Society.

An experienced teacher, Cookie has taught at the Los Angeles Arboretum, San Diego Botanical Gardens, Containers of Our Culture (Visalia, California), Weekend in the Gardens (Quail Gardens, San Diego), Great Basin Basket Makers (Reno, Nevada), Arizona Basketry Guild, Rancho Los Cerritos historic site (Long Beach, California), Harmony Works (Redondo Beach, California), and Artisan Lair (Long Beach, California).

She has exhibited in many galleries and guild events, including Gualala Arts Center (Gualala, California). Cookie regularly encourages other artists to find their own "basketry voice." She currently teaches private students and workshops in her own home studio.

MARLA HELTON

Following a path that began in 1988 with a simple basket-weaving class, Marla Helton began exploring unique combinations of mixed media art forms that incorporates weaving techniques with pottery and gourds. In 1990, she began exhibiting at prestigious juried art shows in the Midwest and selling in art galleries. Marla teaches at retreats, conventions, and galleries all over the country. Marla and her partner, Stuart Fabe, have a studio in

rural Indiana where they find inspirations in their surroundings.

Talking to Marla about her work, she says: "Gourds are a medium that directly affect the approach I take with my weaving. Each gourd has a unique color, texture, and shape that suggests a certain path that will bring forth a special beauty when woven. Exploring various weaving techniques and materials allows each gourd to become a unique sculptural piece that has spirit and soul of its own."

Marla's work has been featured in many publications including: *Weaving on Gourd, Fine Arts Gourds, Coiling on Gourds, New and Different Materials for Weaving and Coiling, Fiber and Gourds, Sunshine Artists*, and *Crafts Report*.

Peggy Hoffman

I was introduced to gourds by Marianne Barnes at a meeting of the Basket Makers Guild in the early '90s. The more I worked with gourds, the more I found what you could do with them. I started weaving on gourds and then painting on them. Wood-burning is my favorite. I have done power-carving, chip-carving, made jewelry, and and there are still so many more things to do with gourds.

Terry Humphries

I spent most of my adult life working as a registered nurse. I started working with gourds after I retired. A friend got me "hooked on gourds" when she invited me to attend a gourd show with her. That was eight years ago. Since then, I spend almost all of my spare time working on gourds. I am the past president of our local gourd patch, and am currently vice president of our state gourd society. I love all aspects of gourd art, but I have to admit, my favorite technique is painting on gourds. I have been painting for almost thirty years. I have now learned how to wood-burn on gourds, and thoroughly enjoy this technique.

Miriam Joy

Artist, teacher, author, inventor, and business owner, Miriam Joy enjoys art with a sincere passion. Being blessed with growing up on the Navajo reservation, where her father taught at the Indian boarding school, gave Miriam Joy an advantage to appreciate Native American Indian culture. That culture also helped her to develop her own style of art, which includes gourd art, jewelry making, painting, and various other art mediums.

When asked what is was like growing up on the Navajo reservation, she likes to sometimes refer to herself as "the little white girl on the Rez" who not only was befriended by the Navajo people, but also was taught to appreciate what nature brings to us all through creating art and the inner peace that goes with it. "I am the happiest when I am creating," she says.

Miriam Joy moved back to Arizona a few years ago where she was influenced again by the big, bellowing, fat-bottom clouds, the turquoise jewelry, the red clay mountains, and the most beautiful sunsets in the world. She knew that, "I had come home."

Having taught craft classes and tole painting for many years, it was the next step to become a full-time artist. Currently, Miriam Joy travels the United States, both teaching and displaying her gourd art using the wax technique that she developed.

Linda Kincaid

I have been interested in arts and crafts my whole life. I have worked with many mediums, including pencils, acrylics, oils, Chinese brush painting on rice paper, and ceramics.

My husband's job took us to Rapallo, Italy, from 1985 to 1987. I was fortunate to be able to take a porcelain painting class in the last months of our time in Italy. The classes were given by a wonderful Italian teacher and were held in the town's fourteenth century castle. We moved to Orlando, Florida, upon our return from Italy and, while looking for a porcelain class, I found a small shop with a vacancy in a class that painted on anything but porcelain. I painted with them for two years. Following that, I painted ceramics in two shops for fifteen years.

My daughter gave me a craft wood-burner for Christmas in 1999 and I discovered a new passion. I was able to teach wood-burning classes part-time at Michaels for five years in Florida and three years in Columbia until they discontinued the classes.

We moved back to South Carolina in 2005 and three years later my sister-in-law gave me a gourd to wood-burn and I found it to be the perfect surface for wood-burning. I now enjoy wood-burning, carving, weaving, and embellishing gourds, as well as making jewelry out of gourd shards.

I joined the South Carolina Gourd Society at the annual Gourd Fest in 2008 and became treasurer/membership chair in 2010. I am a member of the Camden Art Guild, Trenholm Artist Guild, and the Cypress Gourd Patch. I have won awards for my wood-burned pictures and gourds from Camden Art, the South Carolina State Fair, and have been juried into several shows and exhibits.

Lee Kline

I am an Army brat and Army wife. I lived in Europe for six years, and crafts were a way to pass the time. I have dabbled in all sorts of crafts to occupy my time while away from my family. I enjoy painting, so gourd art was easy. Classes at the Gourd Retreats Southern Style over the years have sparked my interests. I expanded to carving, etching, weaving, and whatever else you could do with a gourd. Gourds are a wonderful medium to work on and endless ideas just pop into my brain with each new gourd I see. I thank my husband, Max, for his support. He has been ever-so patient when I get on a roll with creative ideas.

Dr. Linda D. Lake

Dr. Linda D. Lake attended Art Instruction Schools in Minnesota, and is a self-taught artist using a variety of mediums, colors, and techniques, including carving and pyroengraving. Juried into several events, she has won various awards and has contributed donations of her art for local causes.

Her work has been included at Art Ability, an International Juried Exhibition of Art and Fine Crafts by Artists with Disabilities, Paoli, Pennsylvania; the Smith McDowell House, Asheville, North Carolina; the Mint Museum of Arts and Crafts, Charlotte, North Carolina; and First Thursday Art Walk, the Healey Building Arts for All Gallery, Atlanta, Georgia.

Local events include Robert Mills Founders Day, Historic Columbia Foundation's 50th anniversary, Columbia, South Carolina; "Unearth, a Celebration" at Saluda Shoals Park, Ridge Spring Art Gallery, and Tapp's on Main Street in Columbia, South Carolina. As a member of the South Carolina Artists Art in Public Places, Lexington, South Carolina, her work is exhibited locally in numerous places.

Dr. Lake is the past president of the South Carolina Gourd Society, hosts the Capital City Gourd Patch in West Columbia, South Carolina, and enjoys teaching workshops demonstrating a variety of techniques.

Louise Leake

I am originally from Connecticut, where my husband and I enjoyed living on a farm and riding our horses. We retired and moved to Deltona, where we had friends and family nearby. This past winter, he succumbed to asbestosis, leaving me to fill my time with exploring ways to use gourds and paint. I have a daughter who still resides in Connecticut and loves it when I send her a gourd for Halloween or Christmas.

I was introduced to gourds through a garden club member who was teaching pine coiling at a local gourd group. I had done pine coiling and vine weaving, which were plentiful in Connecticut, but found that gourds were the perfect material to weave on for me. I am also a bead weaver, so gourds proved to be a great way to use my beading skills.

I have extensive training and experience in all forms of art and have studied with some nationally and internationally known artists. Since discovering gourds, I have met some incredible gourd artists and have been inspired by their works. I am the past patch leader of the Seminole Gourd Patch where occasionally I teach a class and have worked on the Florida Gourd Show for the last four years. I enjoy making gourd baskets and working with natural materials. I carve, wood-burn, and will experiment with different stains and dyes to achieve interesting textures. My favorite subject for adorning gourds is anything natural: birds, plants, insects, animals, and marine life, all native to the Americas.

Maggie LeDuc

I was born in Toronto, Canada, and came to the Southern California area when I was five years old. I attended grammar, high school, and college in Southern California. My main interest in school was competing in team and individual sports, where I was able to excel. I obtained my Master's Degree in physical education and started teaching at the high school level in the area before securing a job at Santa Monica College, where I taught physical education classes and coached numerous teams. I went back to school in 1986 and received a Master's degree in social work and combined teaching and counseling while at the college.

My interest in the outdoors occurred through athletics and working in a Camp Fire's girls camp at age twenty. Working at the camp was a life-changing experience. I was able to see the mountains and experience nature, clear skies, stars at night, and streams to cross. My life had been spent in the city and now I was free and connecting to nature. Every summer after my camp-counseling experience, I would travel and visit other states, countries, and meet lots of different people in their own cultures and environment. I would take my backpack, sleeping bag, and off I went. I loved being free and in the natural beauty that surrounded me every day.

Growing up, my experience in the art world was non-existent. I was under the impression that to be an artist, one should be able to sing, dance, draw, paint, or play a musical

instrument, which I could not do. I never believed that I had any artistic talent until someone told me that the way I taught my students, the way I gardened, how I worked with people, and the photographs I took of my travels were an art unto themselves.

I took my first pine needle basket workshop at the Long Beach Nature Center in 2004. I had always loved projects and working with my hands. The opportunity to work with pine needles and make something out of them intrigued me. That was the start of, little by little, coming out as an artist. I loved working with colors, natural fibers, and different shapes and seeing a project to its completion. It has definitely pushed a lot of old negative buttons, but I kept telling myself to show up, have fun, and be willing to try new things. On this journey, I have been blessed with some wonderful mentors and teachers, both in basketry and gourd art.

Deborah Carlisle Mann

Deborah Mann joined the Palmetto Gourd Patch in Lyman, South Carolina, in 2010, combining her lifelong interests in knitting, quilting, jewelry, and crafting into a new medium of gourds. A native of South Carolina and a graduate of Clemson University ('80), she has spent over thirty years as a computer engineer for Texas Instruments and then Wells Fargo.

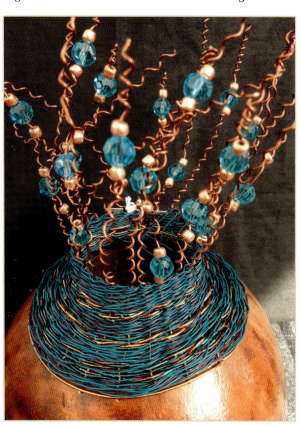

Paul Morris

In October 2011, I was looking for gourds to make birdhouses and discovered gourds were not easy to find. Word of mouth finally got me to a gourd festival in Cedar Mountain, where I discovered the wonderful world of gourd art. I was like a kid in fantasy land and could hardly wait to try my hand at this new craft. I did and was hooked. I have completed many works that I am proud of and continue to enjoy the art and the folks associated with it.

Chris Pace

I was born a "Navy Brat" in the early 1950s at the Great Lakes Naval Base in Illinois. Mother was a registered nurse from Minnesota and father was from North Carolina. I won my first award for art in sixth grade for a fire-prevention poster. There isn't a time I can remember not drawing or doodling on my school papers, much to the chagrin of my teachers. During high school art classes, I was given the opportunity to play with many mediums from clay and pastels to various paint mediums. I always went back to acrylic paint as my first choice, which is where it remains today.

I worked for UPS in the sign shop, doing hand-numbering of postal distribution boxes and on post office windows. This was in the Washington, D.C. area, where we lived after my father retired from the Navy. No official art training was ever offered to me and, other than a few local junior college seminars, I am self-taught.

I moved to Hendersonville, North Carolina, in 1976 and worked for the Council on Aging and then in Medical Records at Pardee Hospital, before moving to Cedar Mountain, North Carolina, in 1990, where I still reside today. I have two grown children and four grandchildren; a fabulous, loving, and supportive husband, Joe, and two cats and two dogs.

I owned and operated my own arts and craft shop in Brevard, North Carolina — "Fox and Berry" — where several area teachers came to teach weekly, both painting and woodcarving. I love carving and sculpting almost as much as I love painting! As a lone painter of cypress knees, I jumped at the chance to travel to Lyman, South Carolina, to meet other gourd artists when friend Lynne Baldwin told me about this fabulous group. Now I am a gourd artist first and a painter/carver of cypress knees second. The fellowship of belonging to a group is very important and encouraging! Each month I learn something new at the Palmetto Gourd Patch and have even taught my style of painting gourd lady pins there. To share with others means you share in someone else's happiness too, which is a blessing I can enjoy a very long time. I ask questions, and I offer tips, and that's where the company of gourd artists is so richly profitable. I host a two-day gourd gathering here where I live called the "Mountain Gourd Gathering" each August.

Patricia Ramsey

Patricia is a gourd artist who attended the Cherokee gathering. Her gourd was won by the author of this book in a fundraiser. She was asked to include her gourd and was thrilled to do so.

Laraine Short

Laraine Short is a member of the National Society of Decorative Painters and president of the local chapter, Decorative Artists of Jacksonville. She is also president of the Northeast Florida Gourd Patch and the Florida Gourd Society nominating committee.

Laraine teaches decorative painting classes at her studio, local and state chapters, art shows, art stores, local and state patches, and state and national conventions. She joined the American Gourd Society and the Florida Gourd Society in 2000. The same year she entered her gourds in competition and won her first blue ribbons for her gourd art. Since then, Laraine received Best of Division in 2003 at the Florida Gourd show, as well as blue ribbons at the Alabama, Indiana, North Carolina, and Ohio gourd shows.

Laraine creates her own designs and has over fifty pattern packets. In the last couple of years, she has added inking, weaving, clay, and burning to the packets. She also has designs in painting books by *Quick and Easy Painting*, Plaid, Sterling Publishing, *Quick and Easy Gourd Crafts*, and *Glorious Gourds Decorating*. Laraine loves to paint and doesn't feel like her day is complete if she hasn't picked up a paint brush. You might find her in her studio around two or three o'clock in the morning with a paint brush in her hand.

Betsey Sloan

A native of New England currently residing in North Carolina, Betsey is the noted author of *InLace Techniques* and *Antler Art for Baskets and Gourds*. She is well known for her teaching of both basketry and gourd art. Betsey has over nineteen years experience in both mediums and runs a successful business selling pods and dried botanicals from around the world.

She is also certified in both PMC and Art Silver. Betsey has taught at the prestigious John C Campbell Folk School, as well as art and craft centers and gourd gatherings from Maine to Florida and as far west as New Mexico.

Patty Snearly

Working with various media has been a major part of my art journey. An undergraduate degree in drawing and painting, a graduate degree in fiber art, and many summers at Penland School of Crafts in North Carolina gave me plenty of opportunities to try various combinations of ideas as well as materials. The last few years I have been painting religious icons. Since this media is very structured, I look to other art outlets for more creativity and imagination. Gourds have been one of my favorites! Since I was first given gourd seeds many years ago, I have been growing and working with them as an art form. They afford me endless possibilities for new ideas and for new uses of old, learned, and practiced skills. I have met so many wonderful artisans over the years and been so fortunate to have gained so much from each experience.

Jack Thorpe

In 1997, a lifelong interest in the arts led to a focus on gourd art after visiting a gourd art gallery. Initially experimenting with wood-finishing techniques, pyrography, weaving, carving, and painting resulted in many well-received gifts to family members and friends. This interest served as inspiration to explore the world of fine art gourds and the refinement of techniques and processes.

Today, this love of gourd art continues, incorporating designs from nature, sculpture, different cultures, and the gourd itself, each gourd having its own unique spirit. In addition to participation in local art fairs and gourd festivals, my work has been exhibited at the following events and galleries: Museum of Latin American Art, Long Beach, California; La Luz Gallery, Long Beach, California; Mesa Verde, La Mesa, California; National Gourd Fine Art Show, The Art and Cultural Center, Fallbrook, California (2001-2002); Lion King Premiere, Los Angeles, California; Guggenheim Gallery at Chapman College, Orange, California.

My affiliations include: Orange County Gourd Society, California Gourd Society, and American Gourd Society.

Lynn Thomas

I live with my husband in beautiful upstate New York in a log cabin we designed and built ourselves. We love the hills, wildlife, and starry skies that surround us. It's a great place to live and to create. The Adirondack Mountains to the north and the Catskill Mountains to the south also speak to my soul and provide great inspiration.

Formerly an art teacher, I am fairly new to gourd art. I "discovered" the idea in 2007 when I came upon a book by Ginger Summit and Jim Widess. I immediately began designing and creating my own gourds and taking my work to craft shows. My gourds can also be found at the Catskill Mountain Artisan's Guild in Margaretville, New York, and at the Broad Street Gallery in Hamilton, New York.

My goal is to continue to develop new designs and techniques and to share my work online and through select galleries and shops. I welcome comments, inquiries, and custom orders.

Lee Tuttle

I have always loved working with my hands and growing things. Gourds are a perfect combination of these two interests. After retiring to Brevard, North Carolina, I was coaxed by a friend to take a gourd decorating class. I was soon hooked and over the years have taken many classes and enjoy learning new techniques. I grow gourds on my farm in Pisgah Forest, North Carolina, and enjoy showing customers pictures of decorated gourds when they say, "What do you do with THESE?" My latest interest is chip-carving on gourds. I belong to the Palmetto Gourd Patch, the South Carolina Gourd Society, and the American Gourd Society.

Angie Wagner

Angie Wagner was raised in a very rural section of Berks County, Pennsylvania, and she continues to live as close to nature as possible. Inspired by the patterns and colors she sees everyday, she works to create symmetry and contemporary forms from chaotic natural materials. She grows and harvests many of the accents used in her work, which led to the name Woven Branch Designs. She specializes in round reed work and gourd art, but is always exploring new materials and techniques. She is a juried member of the Pennsylvania Guild of Craftsmen and her work has won awards and has also been included in galleries and exhibitions. She teaches and writes patterns and her work has been included in several books and magazines. Operating The Country Seat, Inc., a basketry, gourd-weaving, and chair seating supply company, with her parents Bill and Donna, keeps Angie immersed in the basketry world everyday.

Don Weeke

Don Weeke has been making baskets and gourds for more than thirty years. He first learned traditional basketry techniques and the use of natural materials from teacher Misti Washington. Five years after immersion in basketry, he discovered gourds. Don continues to explore the primary focus of his work, form and texture, by combining gourds and natural materials with basketry and, as necessary, invented techniques. His work can be seen in numerous publications such as *The Complete Book of Gourd Craft* and *500 Baskets*. His work is in the permanent collection of American basketry in the Racine Art Museum, Racine, Wisconsin.

Debbie Wilson

Gourd art is something I "fell into" after basket weaving for several years. I took one class on weaving with gourds and I was hooked as a gourd head. I could see endless possibilities for this hard-shelled natural object. I have woven; wood-burned, carved, imbedded objects, inserted metal and painted on gourds for close to ten years, all the while still learning what can be created with these unique forms from nature. My recent endeavors have included experimenting with different effects I can get with stains and dyes and their chemical properties. Carving, is perhaps, my favorite way to enhance a gourd. I like to get really detailed and create textures with different carving bits. Gourds will speak to you and let you know what they are intended to become. Recently retired from teaching art in Greenville County, South Carolina, I am busy still learning what the possibilities are.

Suppliers

The following is a list of the suppliers I use for most of my gourd and basket supplies.

AMISH GOURDS
P.O. Box 21972
York, PA 17402
877-843-0770
www.amishgourds.com

ARNIE'S ARTS 'N CRAFTS
3741 W Houghton Lake Dr.
Houghton Lake, MI 48629
Customer Support/Phone Orders
1-800-563-2356
www.basketpatterns.com

BASKET WEAVING.COM
www.basketweavingsupplies.com

THE BASKET MAKER'S CATALOG
1-800-447-7008
www.basketmakerscatalog.com

BASKET, BEADS, AND GOURDS
Judy Wilson
www.judywilson.com

BAYOU GOURD FARM
www.bayougourds.com

B & B GOURDS
1092 Stillwell Road
Springfield, GA 31329
912-754-3539
zett@windstream.net

Blue Whale Arts
www.bluewhalearts.com
603-679-1961

BONNIE GIBSON'S ARIZONA GOURDS
www.arizonagourds.com

THE CANING SHOP
Jim Widess
1-800-544-3373
jim@caning.com | www.caning.com

FLORIDA PINE NEEDLES
Barb Nelson
www.artgalstudio.etsy.com
artgal@mindspring.com

GHOST CREEK GOURDS
Dickie and Linda Martin
2108 Ghost Creek Road
Laurens, SC 29360
864-682-5251
www.ghostcreekgourds.com

GRATIOT LAKE BASKETRY
5484 Petermann Lane
Mohawk, MI 49950-9612
www.gratiotlakebasketry.com

GREG LESTER FARMS
www.Gourdfarmer.com

H.H. PERKINS CO.
www.hhperkins.com

LENA BRASWELL'S GOURD FARM
Route 1, Box 73
Wrens, A 30833
706-547-6784

MIRIAM JOY GOURD CREATIONS
928-499-9637
Art@MiriamJoy.com
www.MiriamJoy.com

ONNO BESIER
(source for gourd cleaning tools)
912-772-3911

PUMPKIN HOLLOW, LLC
Darrell and Ellen Dalton, Owners
671 CR 336
Piggott, AK 72454
870-598-3568
http://www.pumpkinhollow.com/index.html

ROYALWOOD, LTD.
517 Woodville Road
Mansfield, OH 44907
419-526-1630 or 1-800-526-1630
www.royalwoodltd.com

SANDYLADY'S GOURD FARM
sandlady@sandlady.com
www.sandlady.com

SUZANNE MOORE'S N.C. BASKET WORKS
130 Main Street, PO Box 744
Vass, NC 28394
1-800-338-4972
www.ncbasketworks.com

SMUCKER'S GOURD FARM
717-354-6118

THE COUNTRY SEAT, INC. & WOVEN BRANCH DESIGNS
www.wovenbranch.com
www.countryseat.com

THE BASKETRY STUDIO
(good source for cedar bark)
281 Mantle Road
Sequim, WA 98382
360-683-0050
www.thebasketrystudio.com/supplies/

THE CANING SHOP
926 Gilman Street
Berkeley, CA 94710
1-800-544-3373
www.caning.com

THE GOURD PILE
229-775-2123

THE POD LADY
www.thepodlady.com

TUBULAR WIRE MESH RIBBON
tubularwiremeshribbon.com

TURKEY BRANCH GOURDS
C.L. and Willene Arnsdorff
Springfield, GA
1-912-754-3779
arnsdorfw@windstream.net

TURTLE FEATHERS
PO Box 1307
Bryson City, NC 28713
828-488-8586
www.turtlefeathers.net

WELBURN GOURD FARM
40635-D De Luz Road
Fallbrook, CA 92028
877-420-2613
www.welburngourdfarm.com

WUERTZ GOURD FARM
2487 E. Highway 287
Casa Grande, AZ 85194
520-723-4432
http://www.wuertzfarm.com/index.html

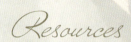

Resources

Books
Devine, Catherine. *Coiled Designs for Gourd Art*. Atglen, Pennsylvania: Schiffer Publishing, Ltd.

Websites
American Gourd Society
www.americangourdsociety.org

BasketMakers.com
www.basketmakers.com
A comprehensive informational site for basketmakers, basket artists, vendors of basketmaking materials and all others interested in the art of basketry. Contact: Susi Nuss

Pine Needles Group
www.pineneedlegroup.com

Wikipedia: The Free Encyclopedia
http://en.wikipedia.org/